Echidna in a Suitcase

The journey through one life

KATHLEEN FRANCES

Published in Australia by Sid Harta Books & Print Pty Ltd,
ABN: 34632585293
23 Stirling Crescent, Glen Waverley, Victoria 3150 Australia
Telephone: +61 3 9560 9920, Facsimile: +61 3 9545 1742
E-mail: author@sidharta.com.au

First published in Australia 2023
This edition published 2023
Copyright © Kathleen Frances 2023
Cover design, typesetting: WorkingType (www.workingtype.com.au)

The right of Kathleen Frances to be identified as the
Author of the Work has been asserted in accordance with the
Copyright, Designs and Patents Act 1988.

All rights reserved. No part of this publication may be reproduced, stored in a retrieval system, or transmitted, in any form or by any means without the prior written permission of the publisher, nor be otherwise circulated in any form of binding or cover other than that in which it is published and without a similar condition being imposed on the subsequent purchaser.

ISBN: 978-1-922958-49-5

About the author

Kathleen Frances lives on the Mornington Peninsula in Melbourne, Victoria. She has two children and a grandson. She has written three other books: *The Adventures of Freddie Hobblesnobble, Tears in a Bottle and Stars on the Sea, Chooking Around: A Story of Keeping Backyard Hens for all Ages 0-100.*

Along with a long career in community services, she has always worked on the premise of optimising her clients' outcomes.

Dedicated to Mum,
who tried so hard.

Preface
When I grow up, I want to be?

When I started to think about writing this book, I had to choose to be honest and peel back the layers that had protected me from events that had no place in my life anymore.

Writing this book slowly started to erode the barnacles that had limited me in different ways for years. Writing to me is a purifying experience and I am in no way a great writer, I am just loving the sense of freedom that comes as you pour your ideas out onto the page.

I was told I have dyslexia and this is something that I have struggled with. I believe it was all trauma-based, as I have become more conscious of the ways my body reacts to things or expresses things, for example. When I go to sleep, my arms are usually on my tummy or by my side as I meditate. At some point in time, they end up over my head like a newborn's. It is as if I am subconsciously doing an above the head wave to some Rajneesh devotee Indian guru. These behaviours are deeply embedded in my subconscious. I may have slept this way after been put in care.

Hopefully my arms were not tied above my head to stop me from moving out of my cot. I will never know: nothing would upset me or shock me anymore. All I know is that the subconscious is a sounder tool than we think. I have other examples of these strange eccentricities, such as clasping one of my hands and gently using my thumb to rub my palm like I am the sea, wearing away at some rough pebble. These are all protective mechanisms that can soothe a small child's psyche from being distressed.

Kids are often encouraged to think about what they will be when they grow up. They have all of those wonderful cues with the most important advocates in their formative years such as their two parents, and, sometimes, siblings. They have people who love and guide them. My start to life as a baby was difficult, my dreams crushed early. I was taken into State Care and my life was never about 'what was I going to be when I grew up,' or about the woman I might become, or the dreams I might have. No. My start to life was about one foot in front of the next, trying to be invisible; to go unnoticed, to basically survive a harsh system that rarely showed any true kindness or love.

Writing this memoir assisted me in an important part of my journey. By piecing this abstract jigsaw puzzle together, it has enlightened me about my innate remarkable sense of self. How do we measure success? Surely not via money or wealth.

Never underestimate a baby growing up and thriving without any parental platform at all. A strong sense of self like mine must have been like a blueprint within my DNA. It has weaved its way all through my life from when I was a small toddler of three to now. These days, the many friends and professionals who know me see a well-balanced capable woman. I see her too. I view myself as a woman who has achieved much. Nothing can change the fact that I was a small, vulnerable baby placed into a children's orphanage, and then, upon departure, into a home with a mentally unwell mother. So, what was I going to be when I grew up? Uneducated. Homeless. At high risk of being a teenage statistic, a single mother with a string of loser boyfriends; a victim of domestic violence. At some point in my life, as predicted, that's exactly what happened.

However, they can put you down, but they can't keep you there. Thankfully, I was blessed with an innate tenacity and a determined temperament. Traits that were always going to propel me through. Like training a vine to an invisible twine, innately I too grew, without twine. I had nothing to cling to except the genetic pool that was within me. I was the random seed you toss in the garden, without nurturing.

Eventually I started to grow and my inquisitive mind grew a little more towards the sun, allowing me to dream. It provided a way for me to disassociate and separate myself from the trauma I experienced. My personality was the very thing that, like the Great Houdini, helped me to escape time and time again. Escapism takes devoted skill. Throughout my story, you will see how I escaped all of the situations that would've completely broken someone else down. Today, because of my malleable spirit, I get up with a bounce in my step and a plan to set small goals. And, when I say I'm going to do something, I mean it 100 per cent. Another thing is, especially after working for twenty-seven years in Community Services in a career where people view others with the analogy, 'Gee she/he had a hard life,' this is not visible with me.

My face is younger than my years. I have a warm smile, and I am told I am attractive with my hazel brown eyes and loving nature. I am welcoming and kind. My close friends are a part of my family. It is important for me to have loyalty and trust and it has taken many years to build close friendships and set good boundaries. The people I truly like and trust, get close. Often any expectations or too many of them frighten me, as I can shy away. If that trust is gone, I back out quietly. At this age I do not have the time or energy to keep being a people pleaser. I left all those insecurities behind many moons ago. Most people see that I have a friendly disposition and this has been a great tool for opening doors up for myself. I actually enjoy my life and this has helped me to stay youthful. This attitude towards life, I can trace right back to the gardens of Nazareth House through to now, along with being so welcomed into a couple of my friends' homes, when I felt so unwelcomed in my own.

By observing and viewing my friends' interactions with their family, I learnt what it is like to feel a part of the whole. These days, when I ask myself, what do I want to be when I grow up, I say, I want to keep learning, daily. I have also learnt that other people's opinions are useless if you do not like yourself. A good teacher is invaluable, I had many. It took a long time to figure myself and my life out. These days, I am glad to have hobbies and many interests such as sewing, cooking, woodworking, creating, travelling, gardening, home-making, writing and beekeeping. Most of all, I want to be a good mother who encourages her kids to have a go. A woman of substance. And I believe that I became all of these things when I grew up.

Contents

Preface	vii
Introduction: Journey	1
Part One: THE ORPHANAGE	**15**
Pegs were made of wood	17
Soldier on!	23
Nesting & prison	33
You are the captain, I am no one	41
No more smoke and mirrors	49
Sounds of silence	55
Cherry red shoes	63
Sunshine On My Shoulders	69
The cocky with Tourette's	77
The garden	83
Daisy dress and picnic day	89
The times, they are a changin'	99

Part Two: LIFE WITH MUM — **103**

Grapes, vines, and bees — 105

Transitioning — 113

Moving from place to place — 119

Mr Bridgewood — 125

Near deaths — 129

The stone angel — 133

Secrets — 141

Smokey — 147

What a day — 151

The bridge — 157

Echidna in a suitcase — 161

Part Three: TEENAGE YEARS — **171**

Brothers, boxing and ABBA — 173

No more eyebrows — 183

A manufacturer's dream — 193

Escaping thunder road — 199

Mum is institutionalised — 205

The shoe factory — 219

The doctor — 229

Moving — 235

Ever after — 247

Part Four: ADULT REFLECTIONS	**261**
Earth angels	263
The boneyard	273
No ordinary moments	281
Woodshedding	289
Forget me not	301
A mother's job is never done	309
Nonna	319
2009: The apology	323
Vines, and calabria	325
My papa	329
Afterword	339
Random Acts of Kindness	339

Introduction
Journey

When I think of why I wrote this book, the analogy of peeling back layers of an onion came to mind. It's used frequently, so I'm sticking with what's familiar rather than coming up with a different vegetable analogy. Many times, I've had to peel another layer from the onion, as painful as it is, or has been; looking back was the only way forward for me. That way, the pain has been dealt with and it no longer has any power over you. When doing my Mental Health Certificate IV, the tutor used a term called *woodshedding*. Apparently, it's jazz jargon and means that you may be seen as not achieving much at all, when, in actual fact, you're succeeding and developing something brilliant and new. It's both a productive and awful thing, but without going through the process I never would've written this book, nor formed my now comprehensive understanding of the frigidity of 1950s society; disproportionate authoritarianism from the church; lack of governmental assistance and social services support, Mum's complex battle with mental health; my ancestry; and myself.

Echidna in a Suitcase, then, is about how quickly things can spiral out of control. How the mental health of a parent directly impacts the children in their care. How the lack of support from the broader community leaves one feeling isolated and disillusioned. How State Orphanages made up their own rules due to the lack of Government agency monitoring. How children learn to be powerless and voiceless (but this no longer has to be the case). How social isolation plagues us all in different ways, and how taking the time to respectfully unpack my suitcases, one after the other, and visit my demons, taught me how to accept my past and learn to forgive. This book is about survival and triumphs and victories won at different stages of my life, and the warmth and love I have experienced throughout.

I had to be brave to open my suitcases, to look inside and re-experience the macro and microcosms that made up my life. There were times when I was at risk of homelessness myself, often living out of suitcases. I think about so many things that writing this book has reminded me of — small compartments that have sat dominantly in the dark, which I opened piece by piece. The more I looked, the braver I became at not only unpacking them, but packing them away where they belonged. The image of the Echidna represented myself at many times feeling alone or aloof on my own journey, prickly on the outside, soft in the middle. Taken away as a newborn, then thrown back into the arms of a mother who was a stranger, a mother who'd lost connection from me and who was struggling with her own severe mental health.

When it comes to multiple traumas, it takes a continual effort and commitment. You truly need to be kind to yourself, and you will eventually get there. Not long after my fortieth birthday, a significant relationship had run its course. The breakup was extremely painful and confronting at the same time. It had been on and off and this was possibly the fault of both parties. As always, I blamed myself and looked for a distraction to move away from the uncomfortable feeling of it finally coming to an end.

I started working on a cheaper rental for the kids and myself. I found a house close to Mornington town centre. It was $150.00 a week rent. It had been abandoned; squatters and homeless people had lived there. It was, let's put it this way, not appealing to anyone other than myself. It was a Californian bungalow- style home, beautiful in its day. No one wanted it the day we did the inspection, but I could see the potential. Eighteen months' cheap rent was the ticket I needed. Even though it was due to be demolished within that time, the kids and I ripped up carpet and exposed old Baltic pine flooring. I scrubbed every inch of this old, forgotten beauty, then I approached the real estate agent. He agreed to pay for some fresh paint. My daughter and I made it look wonderful with a new lick of paint. My friends loved the house. It had plenty of character, that's for sure.

The place was warm, liveable, and super close to town, so both kids could get to and from school on a bus. It was a godsend, financially, as I was struggling to pay off a block of land in Mornington and high rent prices at the same time. At that time, it was hard trying to establish myself in a new location within my career in community services, as you need to have a good grasp on the linkages and other service providers in the local area. I was not so familiar with this. The plan was to build a new home, the kids and me, as it wasn't the first time I had achieved this on my own. In the end, I came to a different decision after struggling to work for the Department of Training and Education, a catering company, and a nursing agency. I had three jobs going simultaneously. I wasn't going to fall into the same traps as Mum had.

I had other issues as a single mother with one child on her teenage journey and my son heading into puberty. I was not doing a wonderful job at parenting my teenage kids; I was missing many links of how to understand teenagers and the challenges that come with this. I was so far out of my depth and definitely struggling with how I should do the best job, the correct thing, not having much of a childhood or guidance through those days on my own. I had no real connection to family, and Mum had just passed away, my only connection to myself. My daughter at times was displaying a true dislike for me. This was all part of the becoming an adult phase. At the time, I was deeply wounded, as she was academically smarter than myself and she was able to make comments that would cut to the bone. That's just teenagers, apparently: like I said this was all new to me.

Then, another transformation came when my daughter turned from a girl who adored unicorns and anything of colour to taking on a completely gothic persona. Like a turtle, she withdrew underneath her tough, protective exterior, choosing her audience and communicating with whom she chose — usually not me! Her multiple academic gifts were always noted by the teachers that taught her: science, music, and on it went (she was gifted). She disliked the seemingly plastic cheerleading girls with no depth. She was more drawn to the arts and philosophy, but this left her isolated and alone, which worried me deeply. Chalk and cheese. Then, my ray of sunshine, my son, who was outgoing and friendly, my saving grace at times, started to assert his strong personality. He was a great sportsman, artistic, musically gifted. He took me on a new journey when he didn't come home some nights.

He needed to be attending places like the famous ESPY, the music forum in Saint Kilda, at sixteen years of age. He presented me with other challenges. I'd lost control of my own children. I was out of my depth. I'd brought both my kids up to be leaders, not followers. Becoming a teenager is dangerous, as I'd learnt. I was so petrified of them getting hurt. This fear led me to places I never thought I would go. I often yelled and was distressed. The more I tried to fix things, the more damaging it was for us all.

I myself was always more of a hippy type, a quirky dresser. My home was eclectic to a degree. I tried to be a cool mum, embrace my daughter's individuality, and acknowledge that cool place in the city, Morticia's. It was positioned, I think, in the Royal Arcade. I was trying to connect. The truth was I hated all the black; it reminded me of the evil, mean nuns I'd encountered as a small child. And then, I tried to support my son when he wanted to sing in a death metal band. Again, I was thrown out of my comfort zone. The Wiccan culture focus and return to the pagan beliefs: boy, I struggled with this at the time. Musicians like Marilyn Manson were all the rage and my son freaked me out as he seemed to be travelling a similar path. I went through a period of not sleeping well. I never slept all night and coping on three hours of sleep was not going well after a few weeks.

Then, after a truthful but painful observation from an

Introduction

ex-partner, I recognised that I was way out of my depth mentally. He said how you could know how to have normal relationships after coming from a family as dysfunctional as your own? Angry couldn't describe how I felt towards him. He had the perfect family. The funny thing is I knew all of this was true. The only connection I ever had was a biological connection to my mother. It was never a deep, emotional, loving relationship and now she had gone, and I'd missed out. There wasn't much keeping our connection together. If anything untoward were to occur, you were thrown out with the dishwater, and this also included my kids. The kids had some support from family, but not like the normal status quo of a normal functioning extended family. I wanted it to be stable, solid, secure and continuous. My mother's death spiritually threw me into a deep dark space as I was already nursing life, and work, teenagers, finances, and a new relationship which again was not healthy. He was emotionally unavailable. My pattern. My stuff to clean up. Grief, the loss of so many things. At the time it was a journey of self-discovery. Who was my father? Maybe I had other family that would love me? Why was I taken away from Mum as a baby? I needed to know things beyond my status of past state ward. How did this come to be? I had many questions. Why?

Ironically, I'd worked in Community Support Services, from 1995 until 2019, a very similar field of work that had been the demise of my family. I wanted to help people, to advance in social justice, and to make small minuscule changes to people's lives, changes that would change the course of their broken lives and repair a part of them to move forward, just a little more than where I'd found them. My first manager, Susie, indicated she had observed me as a support worker. She said I had a natural ability of engaging with people from all walks of life. I found it easy to prelude into clients' psyches with my easy-going approach. This way of getting clients to engage is useful when change is about to occur. By taking the time to assist and support the most vulnerable, I had tapped intuitively into some of the toughest clients' lives.

I taught myself client-centred approach practices way before they became the new buzzword in the community services world. I enjoyed the problem solving and had an abundance of energy when it came to great outcomes. In my own life, I was smooth, and optimised many outcomes if I needed a problem solved.

If I needed something, in some way it would be sorted and it would happen. Yes, I was always a mover and shaker, a person who was focused on all and every task I needed to achieve. When I came to apply for my state ward files, it was harder than I'd expected. It was like ripping gauze from an open wound. It stank. It oozed. It was painful. Within seconds of talking to the insensitive public servant, I was transported back to being humiliated by the mean Catholic nuns and other forms of authority.

When I left the orphanage, there was no clear measuring tool as to where I might be scholastic-wise. I'd only been through kindergarten, and I never remembered school there at all. Also, Mum forgot what year I was born in, and so after being returned to her, she instantly made me a year older. I never attended school until I left institutional life, and I was popped straight into grade two. I wasn't able to concentrate. I had a form of the jitters, coupled with a form of dyslexia. All through my fragmented education, this learning disability added to a huge fear of expression, which kept me from putting up my hand up and asking important questions. If the teacher looked at the fidgeting girl at the back of the room, I would cringe with anxiety or dread. Many times I would be made an example of by the Catholic school nuns.

'Up the front, Kathleen. Sit there if you cannot concentrate, your fidgeting is distracting others,' they'd say.

And, if I needed to get to the toilet, they would make me wait, which was personified by more humiliation as a puddle sat under my chair when I could no longer wait until the bell rang. The fear of humiliation, coupled with the fear of physical pain, taught me to stay unseen and unheard, invisible, and seamless if possible. I was trying to keep under the radar.

But, in real life, that was never going to be a reality for me, coming from what is classed as a lower socio-economic family. Although clean, I was always the daggy-looking one, super skinny, dark-skinned, and awkward, with one sock lacking elastic and the other hiked up with an elastic band. For many years I struggled to fit in at all.

By grade five, I'd created my own learning technique. I'd write things down in my own language for me to process later. And then, I'd break the lesson down into small segments for me to understand. This helped me to learn. I still do this today. Write it down, then revise. I try different approaches customised to a style of learning that has worked for me and has enabled me to build confidence. Challenging myself often sowed the strongest seeds for harvesting. With writing this book, I struggled with writing the first draft myself. Is it me? The girl? She? Me? I felt like the faces of many phases: a girl, a teenager, a woman, a saint, a soul who at times had no belief in her own abilities. Here I was trying to tell a story and not knowing what 'person' to assume. It was a very hard thing for someone to achieve when they missed many steps in their early life and in education and early years of learning. Of course, it has taken many years for me to be honest in expressing that I have dyslexia coupled with ADHD, as well as big gaps in my education.

Mostly, I am an auditory learner, and yet I do love to read

books. I love the smell of a new book as it engages my sensory and auditory receptors. Hearing and reading stories are an absolute joy to me, no matter how the delivery comes. I enjoy the richness of people's compositions and how they can write so easily and express their life stories as they unfold on paper. My life experiences have given me a unique insight into love, loss, separation from love, the opportunity to be a mother, and a new beginning as a grandmother. This is because I was unable to have the first and foremost nurturing from infant to child and wasn't able to mirror emotions and other measurement tools that most children have. Without one strong personality to help build myself from the ground up, I learnt how to gauge these emotions all on my own. The one thing I do like about myself is that I am resourceful and extremely inquisitive, which has given me some really good skills in life and the ability to achieve something, from the smallest goals to the largest achievements.

I also learnt a way to deal with the patterns of trauma in my life. Patterns always play a role in the lives of someone who has lived with trauma. Now, in my fifties, I've found keeping away from certain triggers works. Experiencing trauma, or even re-experiencing those past traumas, as is the case with those who live with post-traumatic stress disorder, brings out many unhealthy components while showing oneself what areas still need to be acknowledged and healed. I live with trauma and, at times, it's been like a friendship. I do try my hardest to move away from unhealthy patterns. I have to engage and commit to change and expect that like any cycle of addiction, there will be times of relapse, but then I pick myself up and start all over again. It gets easier. Just for the record, I'm not talking of drug addiction or alcohol. These have never been an issue for me. Out of eight children in my family, only one used alcohol as a crutch or prop stick. Trauma has been definitely prevalent, though. My only true addiction is drinking my tea; or, as my son mentioned one time: *Mum if we took out the sugar, tea might not be your vice.* Definitely some truth in his comment. Neither of my kids have addictive personalities. Trauma does not always end in addictions.

The good thing is, over the years, I've slowly been chipping away at a new view, a new vista for my life. Nothing will ever be the same. Traumatised people often feel comfortable staying in the similar and familiar situations that they know. To be truly committed is what is needed to move forward. I found my own techniques to help myself, which assisted me throughout my life. Random acts of kindness, and metaphorically speaking, taking my head out of my arse to do something, anything, to learn. Community houses, op shopping. There are so many affordable ways of getting out these days. Most of all taking micro-steps and being gentle on myself has helped. And nowadays, I have fewer stresses to concern myself with. No more single parenting. House paid off. Life is less pressured. I work part-time. No more multiple jobs.

We all become tired of the same old patterns. I couldn't keep listening to my older sisters' version of events, so I decided to break free from their interpretation of my life and discover the truth for myself. This was the hardest journey of committing to counselling and looking at the past until it served me no longer. For the first time ever, just before Mum died, I wanted to do the investigative work, to look back, to explore my humble beginnings and inspect my life closer up than ever before. And, what a journey I've been on. The most amazing outcomes came from looking back; my life will never be the same ever again. While trying to lose my past, I discovered parts of myself that had been hidden. Finding them has now taken me into a brand new chapter of where I belong, and most importantly, to whom I belong. I have transformed from a painful, lonely child to a woman who now embraces and looks forward to other unforeseen changes in my life. Who knows where they might lead?

Part One

The Orphanage

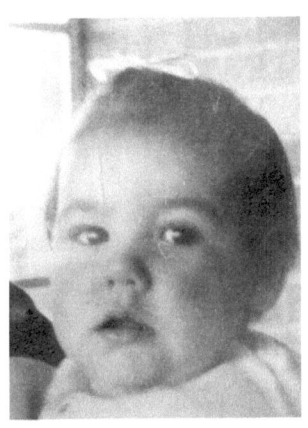

*Myself as a baby in Catholic
Orphanage in Ballarat-Sebastopol
1963*

Pegs were made of wood

Mum told me that during the day before I was born, she was restless, and while sweeping the old, wooden floorboards, a powerful wind blew the door open, startling her, and bringing in the autumn maple leaves from the tree outside. She went into hospital that afternoon. According to the records, I arrived just past midnight that autumn morning, not knowing my arrival would be unwelcome to any of my family, more specifically, Mum's mother. I later understood this as being because of the strong, moral compass my Nana aligned with, and how she could never come to terms with her own frustration and anger about her daughter having had an illegitimate baby by a man of olive complexion, a baby she adamantly wanted to keep separate from her other, more welcome, grandchildren.

I imagine in the wee hours of that morning, just before Mum closed her eyes to sleep, she looked out through the window of her room to see the dawn breaking and the autumn leaves tearing away from their trees to carpet the cold ground, and perhaps, just for a brief moment, Mum relished the safety of those hospital walls, and rested. It wouldn't be long until she would leave the security of the hospital to face her responsibilities. Mum's grandmother, my great grandmother, being a liberal thinking woman and living in the U.K, tried to help prevent her from anymore unwanted pregnancies by sending her the pill before the two boys were born. Mum enjoyed her relationship with her father's mother, cherishing her letters; however, she indicated that when those tablets arrived, they were broken into pieces after their long postal journey. Mum had probably never been offered the contraception pill by her local doctor. He knew all the families in the small country town, tended their coughs, delivered their babies, and nursed their palliative needs. Well-informed when it came to the Catholic doctrine. He was guided by his beliefs and views, I imagine. In 1960s society, women had little say over their bodies, as this would be seen as a sign of power. As long as women were of healthy weight and child-bearing age, they could carry a child.

Also, during this period, there were too few female doctors, what with the limited opportunities for women to go to, or even be accepted into, the more male dominant programs at university. Areas like science and medicine were the hardest to gain entrance to, and if they did, acceptance was often gained only by male vote. This was the case for Dr Elizabeth Blackwell, the first women of the nineteenth century to receive a medical degree in the United States and gain medical registration to the General Medical Council within the United Kingdom. So it was men who generally dealt with women's anatomy, certainly not the anatomy of their spirit, and many women were over-loaded having multiple births over many years, and struggling. This was the case for Mum. Not only that, it turns out I was 'different' from the others. Words straight from the family doctor's mouth. Meaning, I had dark hair and an olive complexion, unlike my two brothers and four sisters. Still, Mum breastfed me just like the previous babies. She didn't care. I was her baby.

She was flying solo. She had little support and was without a breadwinner. The last thing she needed was a new baby to look after. Already with limited money coming in, caring for me left her without a cleaning job, leaving her, and, us, financially vulnerable. My understanding was that because her only husband left her with the four girls, and wouldn't divorce her, she wasn't eligible for certain government support cheques. As I later found out while reading the Widows Pension Act of 1942, there were certain criteria women had to meet to be eligible for the pension. Even though Mum's husband had deserted her and by right, she should've been entitled to the pension, there were certain disqualifications based on character. The act actually states, 'a person shall not be granted to a widow ... unless she is of good character and deserving of pension...'

This meant that between 1947 and 1973, before the legislation changed, women, including Mum, were at risk of either adopting their babies out or becoming financially vulnerable, with their only support being the basic child endowment payment. Some women tried to abort. Mum was one of them. Socially, Mum knew her situation was not the best and I believe if she were able, she would've gone to the city to organise a backyard abortion. There are plenty of stories of females who put their lives at risk to save face during those pretentious times. Instead, she resorted to a cheaper way of forced abortion by throwing herself from the top of the dining room table.

Imagine her bruising and the sheer desperation she must've been under to do this to herself. Its mind-blowing for me to visualise, and yet I was the unborn baby within her womb. I understand she tried other medieval forms of abortion, including having boiling hot baths with Epsom salts; however, I stayed firmly planted within her womb.

As an adult, I have empathy for the miserable situation she was in. Women died awful deaths by putting themselves in terrible danger going to backyard butchers, the knock shop, all for saving face in communities like the one I was born into. Younger women were quickly shipped off to hospitals and places hidden away from society. Some of these places were like baby factories for people who were desperate to adopt a child. These places gave the adopting parents choices, while the young mothers had none; they were left to hide their loss, their pain, and their past.

How do I know this? Mum yelled it at me as a child. Blow-by-blow accounts that often left me feeling distressed and unwanted. How very alone Mum must've felt taking herself off to hospital to give birth to me. Was she focusing on the isolation? She had no one to support her in the birth suite and there was not a soul in the waiting room anticipating the baby's sex, no father waiting with a beautiful spray of flowers, no anxious mother bearing the weight for her daughter. She was alone, and I suspect she would've been aware of the shame weighing heavily upon her. Let's face it, Mum had already given birth six times before. There were no happy endings, and this was her gig alone. I can only imagine that as the labour pains intensified, she must've been at the point of no return. Nothing could be avoided now, the awkwardness, the gossiping, and the small-town folk doing what they'd always done — crossing the street and whispering about her, and her now brood of seven!

Soldier on!

Mum came from a hard-working, tight-knit family who managed through the times of the Great Depression. Surrounded by this strong nucleus with a rock-solid connection, I presume she'd been given a morally strong upbringing from which she gained a solid sense of self. Her father was born in 1893 in the Parish of Riddings, via Derbyshire. He had emigrated from England during the First World War. Mum's mother's family had come from Ireland, a generation before her father's family arrived. The story goes that somehow, both being horse lovers, my grandparents met at the Royal Melbourne Agriculture show. Apparently, Nana was a keen horse rider and loved horses, as did my grandfather, who had been a jockey and horse trainer. They were married at Saint Mary's Catholic Church in Ascot Vale, Victoria, on the 28th March 1919, although if my grandfather hadn't converted to Catholicism from the Church of England there possibly wouldn't have been a wedding.

Nana was a staunch, devout Catholic. Her God lived at the opposite corner down the road from the hotel. She was a no-nonsense kind of woman with the backbone of a mallee bull. Mum barely spoke about her mother, hard and unapproachable. There was an unwritten tension between them, and I certainly felt the coolness. Nana was said to be very strong-willed; she did not suffer fools. She had a high moral bookshelf where she kept all her unyielding views, and no one dared question her authority. Once she spoke, it was final. My grandfather was on the troopship Ballarat on the 17th of April 1917, which was torpedoed in the English Channel. Apparently, he was too busy gathering his personal belongings when the ship was bombed and was ordered to get off the ship! He must've done so without a stitch of spare clothing or item because he survived the situation. He indeed struggled after the war for the rest of his life.

My research shows his service was in the British Army for 717 days. He was discharged on the 28th of April 1920 for the reason of a gastric ulcer. Sadly, the Australian government wouldn't grant him a war pension, after all the stress of serving and suffering from many ailments. He pretty much worked up until his death.

Mum was born in March, 1924. She already had a brother

two years older. He was born in 1921. Another brother followed in 1927. Mum's words were kind when she spoke of her father. She said he was a kind and caring man, and a loving father who told her she was his only girl. She told me stories of him and her at the Flemington Racecourse. He'd hold her up over the racetrack barrier so she could see Phar-Lap, the famous horse, training. Mum said they'd go to the track by horse and jinker cart and that one day, when they were coming into the city, my grandfather's brother also came over from England after he'd fought in Gallipoli. My grandfather, seemingly, was amazed his brother came home physically uninjured. He also married and had a son and two daughters.

In any case, Mum felt much love and she was. She was surrounded by a loving family. Mum's nickname was Peggy because pegs were made of wood back then, and her maiden name was wood, so she was affectionately known as Peggy. She was the glint in her father's eye, with two brothers who adored her. Sadly, due to a very tragic unforeseen accident, Mum, at seventeen or so, woke up one morning to find both her brothers had been involved in a collision with a car after leaving a country dance. It was the 9th of July, 1943, and the brothers were on a big German motorcycle. They had a very good friend on the back. Tragically, the three boys hit a car, or were hit by a car. The facts are still unclear. Two brothers were dead within the week and the friend was holding onto his life in the Sale Regional Hospital. According to the coroner's inquest, they were never able to solve the conundrum of who hit who.

From this moment things seemed to change for Mum. She endured the worst emotional pain that a young teenager could experience in their life, enduring immense loss and grief. She'd lost her support system, her protectors, her escort to dances. They were gone! My poor grandfather was distraught, and according to Mum, he had to be strong and go the mortuary of McIntosh and Co. The coroner's report noted his words when he stated, 'I have now seen the body of my son, Sydney, in mortuary of McIntosh and c/o. He is twenty-two years old. His usual occupation is as a Bench Press.' And again, 'I have now seen the body of my son, Clementine Patrick. He is in mortuary of McIntosh and Co. He was a tally clerk. I last saw him alive at 6.30am on the 8th of July, 1943.' Reading the coroner's inquest, I felt devastated for my grandfather, a man who also died much earlier than expected. The attendant at the mortuary asked, 'Is this your son Clement, a bank clerk?' Sadly, he replied, 'Yes'.

This tragedy bore down hard on a usually united family. It's been said that Mum awoke to her mother's screams of 'Not my boys!' which any mother in this situation would've done. She was very upstanding and respected within her small community and was highly involved in her children's lives. Acceptably, she became over-bearing and far too protective of Mum, which I suspect left her emotionally stunted at the ripe age of eighteen. Being so sensitive, Mum couldn't bear the weight of the grief and the social consequences, as if grief were a curse. She indicated how the people living in their small country town would become awkward when they saw her, crossing the road instead of acknowledging her at that time. She said they'd always be murmuring or whispering or saying, 'There's she goes, that girl; you know, her brothers died tragically,' or something of a similar vein.

Mum's mother had changed too, and who could blame her? Her losses were as traumatic as Mum's. Their hearts had been broken, not one time, but multiple times. Nana's beautiful boys were gone in one fell swoop. The house was full of silence and sorrow and silently and inwardly Mum wished it had been her instead of the boys.

The reason I say this is because my family is gifted in having visions. I too have this gift, as does my daughter. Mum told me she had a terrible dream the night before the accident and instead of them, she was on the bike. She often attended the dances with the boys, as they would chaperone her and keep an eagle eye out for her, especially Sydney; he was three years older and at that time had already enlisted in the army. Mum idolised her brothers. She indicated how much she loved her little brother, saying he had the face of an angel. They both were young, very close, and ready to serve their country and crown in their army uniforms, dignified and dedicated.

Mum mentioned there was talk of a couple who were parked on the Princes Highway in the dark at the time when the boys had the accident. The streetlights were out because of the fear of being bombed. In Australia, lights out during the Second World War was known as the brownout, different to the blackout that occurred in London and the UK. In Australia, there were many fatalities due to poor night vision. Looking at the archives, there is mention of car wheels. Why didn't this couple assist or help in some way? Instead, the boys were left lying on the road. My youngest uncle died on impact. His brother was still alive, and Jacky J, their friend, was also knocked unconscious. When Jacky woke up, he had only a faint memory of my uncle Syd saying, 'Not far now, Jacky, we're nearly home.' Those were the last words he heard from my uncle. Jacky had survivor's guilt, and later had a battle with the booze. He'd also been an attractive young man, even in his older years. But like Mum, whose mind eventually became distorted and far from reality, shattered like thousands of shards from a broken mirror, the trauma of this event impacted him for the rest of his life. Mum became aware that her mind was not the same, and I believe this would have been the start of her own trauma.

Not long after her brother's deaths, Mum married an acquaintance of theirs. She must've been smitten with her new man, and I imagine the feeling was mutual. They looked so beautiful together. He was tall and attractive with hazel eyes, and Mum was the vision of a Hollywood movie star with her long blonde hair and eyes as blue as the sky above. Even so, unknowingly, Mum had married a man with a predestined anxiety issue. Then after serving in New Guinea during the war, he ended up with war neurosis. With the war ending in 1945, many men came back severely changed. Many times, families were torn apart by the pressure to begin again and the consequent effects of post-war trauma, which for some veterans included self-medicating through comradery and drinking. Many men stuck to a code of honour, meeting with comrades at the local hotels and RSL. However, this familiarity would eventually become a place for them to hide their unrelenting torment and to deep dive into the bottle, a release from the pain. There were two places in town to find atonement, or peace, both on the same street. One was the church and the other was the local pub. He chose the pub.

Following these drinking sessions, with anger fermenting up to burst, some of them went home and beat on their wife or children, loved ones who became outlets for hidden and voiceless problems. Mum was one of these unsuspecting wives with a husband who subjected her to further pain, deepening her emotional grief. Perhaps she hoped this man might replace the love and attention she so missed from her brothers. I suspect the violence she endured during this relationship added to her progressively fragile constitution. Times were tough.

She'd coped with the pregnancies and births of his four girls like a trouper, but in those latter years of their marriage, he would disappear for months at a time. No one could locate him. Mum worked menial jobs and received a small payment from the Clerk of Courts. Cheques were sent by post, usually. Even then, with four kids in her care, she was experiencing financial struggles, as he would leave her on her own with the girls for long periods. She would not know where her husband was, or when he would be back. She must've realised in the end that his alcoholism and abuse was too much to deal with. She hung in there till the early 1950s when she decided enough was enough. She wanted a divorce, but he wouldn't let her get on with her life. It wasn't that easy. Now knowing about the hard judgment upon women's characters by the welfare system, I suspect that her not being able to achieve a divorce held Mum back from obtaining a proper pension. If she'd been allowed the Widow's Pension, perhaps the coming events would've been less traumatic. Perhaps, Mum would've kept afloat and kept her children. In 1954, after being abandoned by her husband for close to four years, Mum unexpectedly met an Irish Catholic man, and she formed a relationship with him.

From what I understand, Mum first saw him playing piano and he sang her a song. He was much admired by all with his charcoal dark wavy hair, and blue eyes. I believe he cared for my Mum, although he never married her. He loved music and possibly a good time more. I believe my mother never truly matured properly mentally from the time her brothers died; the trauma had changed her neural pathways. I know she suffered greatly. I believe she was unable to problem solve, or see how vulnerable she was until it was too late. She said her mother took to him easily, approving of their friendship. He never married, and died in 1972. This being the case, he probably never knew that his two boys ended up in state care. Once her relationship with my brothers' father ended, Mum was left with six kids in her sole care and a declining mental state. She was still struggling financially and, I believe, had started to often self-medicate.

I wouldn't say Mum was ever an alcoholic, as she didn't attend hotels frequently, but I think in 1961, for a woman to be seen once or, god-forbid, twice in a hotel was enough to start the gossips. It wasn't hard for a woman to form a reputation of loose living without meaning to. Mum was a good person; however, by this time, she'd had children ranging from the oldest at eighteen years to the youngest at four. Her behaviour was socially unacceptable and frowned upon, not only by her own mother, but by other women in the local community. Sadly, by this time, her father had passed away. He'd really been her only significant male support and role model. Who knew what levels of grief Mum was dealing with? Let's put it this way: Mum, asserting her right to have an alcoholic drink or attend a dance, was never going to be seen as a good thing in a small rural community. And, from what I understand, my older siblings and my nana felt humiliated by her actions.

Nesting & prison

As an adult, when you look back and see things that happened to you, you realise just how important and informative those moments were. Also, through writing this book, there have been many things from my childhood and life that resurfaced, coming back to me as small pieces of information from the compartments of my sub-consciousness. Having sat all these years waiting in the dark, they were ready to reveal my reality. I dug deep and found the courage to face my demons, accept and integrate them, and then finally pack them away. I thought I had no complete understanding of how I came to be, although, writing this book has helped me to fill in the gaps. Pieces of the puzzle were also collected through counselling therapy and while working as a social worker. Counselling made an enormous difference in helping me to come to terms with my childhood and to reframe my understanding of Mum and why she made certain decisions.

Furthermore, through my vocation as a social worker, I've been able to acknowledge historical elements of society, including the pressures which directly impacted Mum's life, after the war and then during the early sixties when I was born. I've been able to make sense of the small mistakes that people make, which seem inconsequential at the time, but in fact can be the undoing of a person. They are like tiny hairline fractures that start out as miniscule problems. Unaddressed, they grow in strength, meeting with other people's irresponsible decisions, and can cumulatively cause immeasurable change to the lives of others, particularly those who've no control over their situation, like children who live at the mercy of their parents or caregivers.

From my discoveries, I can only conclude Mum fell victim to such disturbances and, consequently, so did my siblings and myself. I don't wish to blame anyone for my life. In fact, I have realised that no one in the end is to blame. We all need to take responsibility for ourselves. The following, then, is my take on my coming into the world.

A few nice compliments and some attention, and Mum seemed to let her guard down. Perhaps she felt she was passed childbearing days, being in her late thirties; perhaps she felt in charge, in control, powerful; perhaps she wanted to throw all caution to the wind, or maybe she was just vulnerable, and couldn't face her realities. As an adult, and learning of how Mum struggled with postnatal depression, low iron, and anaemia, I can now understand how the smallest and simplest of problems could have escalated, unravelled, and become out of control. That is what happened to Mum, and consequently to us all.

Mum tried to keep herself financially afloat by taking cleaning and other menial jobs, and she'd tried to make contact with her sons' father; however, he was nowhere to be found, just like her husband and father to the four girls. None of these men acted responsibly, or emotionally, towards their kids. They also didn't assist financially. Even though we were poor, Mum kept a clean home, and she must've been caught up in the sales pitch from a door-to-door Electrolux vacuum cleaner salesman who tempted her with this amazing, magical piece of new machinery, which ultimately cost her dearly. Clearly, Mum didn't do her maths, but you can bet the salesman was not out of pocket on point of sale. She signed on the dotted line, and he received his monthly retainer.

She couldn't really afford a vacuum cleaner, so she bought one on finance terms. Apparently, she was paying this off at fifteen pounds a month. Mum was only able to receive fortnightly part payment of child endowment payments, which was twenty pounds back then and was the equivalent to present day four weeks of low income. These cheques would come in the mail. However, one day, the cheques stopped coming. I'm told that Mum went to the Clerk of Courts to advise them she hadn't received the cheques for about a month or two and that she was falling behind in her rent and other payments, including paying off the vacuum cleaner. The Clerk of Courts wouldn't write her a counter cheque to cover the payments she hadn't received, and she left them that day empty handed.

Around the same time, two local policewomen were keeping tabs on Mum. Although, she was a law-abiding citizen, she was struggling to feed seven hungry mouths and may have begun to look interesting to the police. I don't know. She was doing the best she could under her circumstances. She wasn't getting any financial support from any of the children's fathers. It's surprising to me that we managed to stay alive, especially when the cheques stopped coming. Now, when I look back, I find it tragic. So much suffering could've been avoided if the postman had done his job, the job he was paid to do: deliver the letters.

Apparently, the local mailman began to dump the mailbags instead of delivering the letters, which is why Mum hadn't received any of her endowment payments, and how she ended up defaulting on her payments for the financed vacuum cleaner. Mum was relying on those cheques to survive. Due to the mailman's incompetence, Mum's situation went from bad to worse and it became the demise of us all. The postman didn't realise how significant his job actually was; the lives of seven children were changed forever due to the power of those undelivered cheques. How the subtle hands of fate dealt my family a losing deal when that mail went missing.

As mentioned prior, there were two head-hunting policewomen chasing Mum's tail. Looking back at the police reports, their suspicions and speculations were real, but I now think, completely unnecessary. The officers painted a terrible picture of Mum. She was not hurting anyone but her own self by this time. I also struggled as a single parent of two children, and there are many insecure women who do think that single mothers might move in on their husbands when, in actual fact, this tends to happen with couples that hang out with their close-coupled friends. I have seen this happen at least six times in my life.

Mum's voice of explanation about her dire situation kept falling on deaf ears. Those local, smalltown policewomen abused their positions of power by keeping tabs on a person who was no threat to anyone in the community. Mum was a law-abiding citizen, clearly struggling to survive, doing the best she could under dire circumstances. Nevertheless, because of the default payments on the Electrolux, Mum was charged by the policewomen, hungry for a conviction, on a miniscule, insignificant charge: defaulting on a fixed payment.

Mum found herself before a judge and was sentenced to time in Fairley's Women's Prison. From what I understand, this 'time' amounted to as little as three weeks, maybe less, which is ironic considering the total time I spent in the orphanage was eight years. Looking back, the punishment my siblings and I endured seems out of proportion with the seriousness of the crime. I could understand if Mum was a murderer or a hardened criminal, but she wasn't. She was a victim of events. She simply couldn't pay off her vacuum cleaner, having not received her endowment cheques.

She found herself in the company of some of Victoria's most hardened female criminals, and no one in my family, including Nana, wanted to care for me, a five-month-old baby. I gather, by the records, I was placed somewhere for a two-week period. During this time, I believe Nana, or someone close, had to make the decision. The same two policewomen not only took me, but they intervened and took three of my siblings. My two older brothers and the youngest of the four sisters from Mum's only marriage.

I was whisked away into an institution in Royal Park, Melbourne, for processing, then three additional other places before going to Ballarat. From the records, I found out Nana also assisted the police, which forced me to wonder if she was hoping that would be the end of me, the 'illegitimate' baby. I believe Nana and my oldest sister did not expect the authorities to take anyone other than the me. The records state I'd already been thrown across a room and was bruised. Yet, at the time, Mum was already remanded in prison. This is what the files read. For all of us five victims, including Mum, life became more painful than ever. The truth is I had two very large birthmarks, one the right side of my upper rib cage and the other lower left side. No bruising at all.

She suffered and underwent the worse humiliation of all: to be disowned by her own mother and her eldest daughters, who were being manipulated by good morals instilled by their grandmother. It's hard to know who truly is to blame for this terrible injustice. Was it the postman for dumping the cheques? Was it the fathers who abandoned their responsibilities? What about the two policewomen for not understanding mum's situation? The Clerk of Courts that turned her away? Mum's religious mother? Or, was it those other family members morally misguided by Nana feeling the pressure to protect their own characters? Does it even matter, anymore? It all ends the same.

A six-month-old baby is made a ward of the state, along with my two brothers and my older sister. Like prisoners in a Jewish prisoner-of-war camp, my siblings and I were numbered. It's a blueprint that will remain in the system long after we are dead and gone.

I am K8135.

Peter is P8147.

Paul is P8148.

Mary is M8136.

You are the captain, I am no one

When my mother died, I began a search-and-rescue mission of my own life. I needed to uncover information about who Mum was and what her life was like. I needed to form my own conclusions about how I came to have the upbringing I did. At the time, I was at the end of the road emotionally. Grief is known to bring up lots of past trauma and this surely happened to me. It was like the valve of a tap was turned on and I couldn't stop it for trying anymore. I began to recollect stories my siblings had relayed. These were often snippets of larger stories, or glib comments they'd made. Memories began to surface, things Mum had said or shouted at me in frustration.

Fortuitously, after her passing, I was working for Vanish. They were an organisation who provided support for people who'd been separated from their family due to adoption. At this time, they were also providing information and support to a group of people called Forgotten Australians. These people, now adults, were all former Wards of the State, taken by the state and involuntarily placed in institutions. While working for Vanish, I listened to stories from some of the men who were placed into care at around the same time my siblings and I had been placed there. I had been placed in a few places, children's homes, the last four years in Nazareth House Camberwell in the mid-1960s.

Piece by piece, memories began to flood into my own consciousness as if the sandbanks holding me together all these years had been washed away in the downpour. It was only through my willingness to investigate their truth that I became brave enough to unpack my own memories fully, look at them, and inspect them for what they were and are. I felt consumed by feelings that everything that had happened throughout my life was simply my fault. I acknowledged that I had some awfully unhealthy behaviours. I mean, we all play our own part in the play, and staying away from triggers worked so much better. As a woman in my fifties who hadn't dealt with the trauma of my childhood, I had a lot of residual feelings that acted out in many unhealthy reactions. Looking back, I consider this to be a rather normal behavioural pattern, considering the amount of trauma I encountered in my young life. Most of my growth only occurred once I moved further and further away from my family, though. It took a few decades to move away from the ongoing patterns that often came from left of field.

One of my new ways of being responsible for myself was to recognise that accepting the reality of my relationships with my siblings was unhealthy and possibly toxic. My decision to distance myself was not from not loving any of them, somewhat the opposite really. I simply grew tired of always protecting myself around them. I was never able to just be myself. I felt, sometimes, their behaviour was both predictable and distressing. This growth caused me to face the truth about my childhood and to apply for my state ward files, not once but twice to dig up my past no matter how disruptive or painful it would be. It was my hope that the information there would enable me to fill in a few gaps. I needed to know things. Who was my father? Why was I taken away?

The day I went to the big DHHS building in Melbourne City, my heart was pounding. I felt I was going to have some big revelation, or worse, that something dreadful might happen. I took the lift, which took me near the top of the building. Upon arrival at the counter, I was met with a very uncaring and abrupt public servant.

'There's the paperwork. Fill it out,' she said. 'Then go to the register. You'll have to pay for the documents.'

I was already anxious, but now I felt mad. Here I was having to pay for a snippet of my life, a piece in the puzzle!

Being tenacious, I turned and said, 'By the way, my name's Kathleen.'

She didn't care. I was provided with no support while filling out what seemed to be mountains of paperwork. I wasn't coping with all the format and question after question, not to mention the emotional upheaval I was going through and then my dyslexia always getting in the way. I started to crack and began to cry. It was then I thought about all the others that would've come before to apply for their files. How hard would it have been for them, too?

It was then I requested a phone number, any number, a lifeline! There must be a service that can assist, I thought. The disgruntled government worker disappeared returning with another hard-face woman who handed the needy me a phone number on a piece paper. In my hopelessness, I found a pay phone. What I didn't know then was that this phone number, or rather the women who I would speak to, would change my life. Crying, I called the number. This was my first introduction to a lady called Wendy Gale. She was amazing, and she pretty much saved my life that day.

She told me, you are not a failure, you are a survivor. That is all it took. She rephrased my thought-pattern by entering different terminology. I was a survivor instead. I was sinking. Well, for a moment. Wendy gave me the lifeline I needed. When it came to suicide prevention, she made me promise to come in and see her the following week. It was then we spoke at length about my experience while applying for my files. Immediately, she tackled this head on. That's how she did things. A no-nonsense, strong woman, an advocate for the forgotten Australians. Then, one month after Mum's death, she invited me to attend the *Senate Inquiry into Children in Orphanages*. My daughter and I went together. We listened to other testimonies, and for the first time, I addressed the senators and told them about my life being like sliding doors.

Next thing, I was invited to travel to all the DHS offices and talk a little about my life and the sensitivity needed when handling us, the state wards, when we apply for our records. My story assisted in some big changes when it came to the application process of applying for your records; this included how state wards could access their records and would no longer have to pay for them. Wendy Gale was the manager of Vanish at this time, and although there were other stakeholders, plus care leavers, all under the same roof, I was offered a position. My role was to organise easy access for brokerage for all care leavers. The only criteria was that they had to have been in care in Victoria. She organised access to sit with a counsellor if applicants needed support when reading their files for the first time.

On receiving my own records, I found many heart-wrenching letters to the authorities from Mum. She'd begged for me to be returned to her. She wrote of how much she loved me: 'Please let my darling baby girl be returned to us as she is truly missed.' She wrote to them of needing to be close to me: 'Could I work at the baby home in Royal Park Parkville for free? This way I could be with my baby. I miss her terribly.' There were many other similar letters. Imagine my surprise at when I received my files. These sentiments were the first time I'd ever heard that Mum had truly loved me. I was incredibly grateful for my files and any other scraps of my life that were included. No words can express the complete sense of integration of the knowledge that I was loved. I had never known a loving, expressive mother.

After we were reunited, Mum struggled with her mental and physical health, and she was abusive. I now know she didn't know any better way of coping with her lot. The experience of Mum's brothers dying as young men, the experience of being disowned by her own mother, the experience of a failed marriage and unstable partners, the time in prison, these life experiences seriously broke her down, as did the many traumatic experiences the Forgotten Children encountered whilst living in the Australian orphanage. My older brother was very protective before he went to the boys' home. He came back to us an angry stranger. When I read the letters, I suddenly realised my life wasn't meant to have been without love. Love had been there all along, but, in the end, my family members were so hurt they in no way could express it.

I'd like to thank Wendy Gale for being so judicious and for being the person who cushioned me when I didn't think I could go on. This is community love in action and through that there have been many positive outcomes of the personal growth. Granted, Wendy and I drank lots of cups of tea and there was the 'odd' tough time. But to have gone through that and to have initiated change for how care leavers received their files is a pretty good feeling. Quiet achievers are the people who do so much good in this world. They don't need a medal or to stand in front of a big audience to be accredited. We need more Wendys in the world, that's for sure.

No more smoke and mirrors

Having gathered much research, I discovered that within the first four months after being taken in by the State that I was moved three times before finally being settled in the then Catholic Ballarat boys' home run by the sisters of Nazareth. These days, this home is notorious for the misconduct and sexual abuse of young persons by many of the clergy. Thankfully, when I was close to two years of age, I was then moved to Nazareth House, which is also run by the sisters of Nazareth. According to their records, I had one annual visit a year for the purpose of recording my milestones. Not one important record was kept from the sisters of Nazareth. Instead of creating sanctuary for struggling families, institutions like the one I was sentenced to seemed to take advantage of families torn apart by an insensitive and seemingly unjust system.

I feel the Catholic Church has been built on the pain and

suffering of the innocent, where no nurturing or love was present. Instead, orphans and state wards were doomed to spend years in violence, isolation and uncertainty at the hands of men and women who had endless opportunity to prey on societies most vulnerable. I experienced the toughness and stoicism of mostly nuns with no generosity of spirit, warmth, or knowledge. These women, who were supposedly close to Jesus, lacked his ability to love the little children. They had no nurturing ability. As an adult, I now understand that many Irish nuns came from poor families, and were perhaps running into the church from their own abuses and tormented pasts by becoming Brides of Christ. These roles, however, only provided other forms of deprivation after they dedicated themselves to the life of impoverishment that the cloister would bring. Then, as young women, living in convents, young nuns would've had to deal with another problem: the convent's caste system, with the church being the power that decides their fate, not God nor Jesus.

From what I understand, the church would often keep the poorer and uneducated nuns in a low caste to live a life of cleaning and hardships. The educated and more prosperous families' daughters would rise up the ranks of the cloister ladder, eventually being promoted into a Mother Superior role; however, many Irish families did not come from a life of abundance. They were very poor, and it makes sense to me that offering a daughter to the Catholic Church cloister to fulfil the role of a nun, would, in essence, make one less mouth to feed. These young women were sent from Ireland to do God's work, and I can only conclude that for some of them, the bitterness never left them. There's no surprise then, that some of the nuns in the orphanage I lived in were aggressive and sadistic, not dissimilar to their male counterparts, who also made life for vulnerable children very disorientating and terrifying. Often young nuns were put in powerless positions, and preyed upon by clergy men, men of faith, men of God, men who rorted their power over others.

There were a small number of nuns who did have sorrow in their hearts and these young women often tried to show some compassion, like one of the nuns who cared for me, Sister Paula. She spent most of her time with the younger children in the nursery and would often tell stories about Jesus and Mary, the Blessed Mother. She had a strong Irish accent and a kind tone to her voice. I now know that the nursey had been somewhat of a safe haven for me. Even though I was not watched at night, I was at least comfortable in the safety of my small cot. I had a few toys to play with and during the day was able to stay with Sister Paula. I had been the youngest at Nazareth House for a long time until Danny arrived. Rest in Peace, Danny Boy. A song for you, my little friend, 'Oh Danny Boy,' by Frederick E. Weatherly.

Not long after Danny arrived, I was placed with all the other older children in a neighbouring dormitory, which was overwhelmingly large compared to the safety of the nursery. Prior to this move, I had minimal contact with the larger part of the orphanage. My new bed seemed far away from everything I'd known. I was going from Sister Paula and Danny to a thirty-bed dormitory where all the beds had matching bedspreads, as if this uniformity would provide a sense of security. On the contrary, I learned early that the congruency in bedspreads only aligned to the consistent abuse that was dished out on a daily basis. To this day, I still remember the room smelling of ammonia or bleach to mask the urine smells. There was a smell I found some comfort in, which was inviting to my senses, being the beeswax used to polish the floors.

Soon after my arrival to the dormitory, I began to learn about fear. I became aware that other children cried themselves to sleep at night while confined in their beds, too scared to get out, left only to imagine where the sharp, scratchy night-time sounds were coming from. We were all afraid. Afraid of the night and the nuns who made up awful stories as a ploy to lock us in our beds. I presume this ensured restful sleep and uninterrupted nights for the nuns. I recall one nun in particular, Sister Agnes, who had a sharp tongue, was overweight, and had a hand that flew from under her black garment like a brutal weapon. She used it often to keep us in line and under control. We all feared her the most. After prayers, she used to tell us tales about a black dog who moved around in the dark. If you were naughty that day and had sinned, you'd better look out because the black dog was sitting under your bed waiting to catch you. Scared out of our wits and fearful of the lurking dog, most of us resorted to bed wetting during the night. It was unavoidable and understandable if you were frightened of being eaten by a hungry, drooling, demon dog with sharp teeth and big jowls.

Sounds of silence

Sometimes, just sometimes, there was a calming hush at night in the orphanage, which I liked. It would appear just for a brief moment before being abruptly broken with a shriek or an unwelcoming sound, which would come as a reminder that nothing was safe. I would imagine how children in normal households went to sleep with a kiss on the cheek and fairy tales and the odd lullaby thrown in for good measure. I suspect they slept peacefully. If they woke up, scared, a parent would be there to reassure them everything was okay. As a youngster I didn't go to bed with such fantasies. As the frightening dark eventually turned into the approaching dawn with its morning sunlight appearing, more stress came with the morning.

Sister Agnus would come to berate the children who had wet the bed overnight. The offending children would often be paraded around the room with a soiled sheet pinned over their heads, often attached to the children's nightie or pyjamas. This was followed by being tormented and teased. I saw Sister Agnus belt the other children many times. On one day, I watched as this nun loosened her thick, wooden rosary from around her midriff, and began to violently wrap the black rosary beads around a small boy's legs, simply because he'd wet the bed. Observing the cross on the beads, I wondered what Jesus would think of all this? I had always stared at this cross in chapel many times understanding early on that Jesus, whose father was God, gave himself away to save humankind.

Either way, there was no immediate salvation for the children at the Sisters of Nazareth. The darkness of the night instilled an uncertainty, while the day brought its routines and rules that must be obeyed. For many, the day never started pleasantly, for there always seemed to be a rotating roster of pain. I never wanted to wet my bed if I could help it. But of course, it was inevitable that I would, and I paid the penalty for my sin. Being a natural problem solver, I began to concoct a plan so that I would not fall asleep and *ever* wet the bed again. I was vigilant with the execution and, truth be told, I hardly had a wink of sleep throughout my early childhood. Fear often kept me awake, for if I wet the bed, I had Agnes to deal with; if I legged it out of bed, there was the demon dog. Either way I was trapped.

One night with no moon out, all was unnerving and quiet when I became desperate to go to the toilet. I was terrified of where the demon dog was lurking and did lay in bed until the pain was so bad that I felt I might burst. I'd strategized with myself many times on how to escape from my bed, but I'd never actually done it. This time, however, I was busting, and so with a plan firmly in place and by building myself up with the affirmation that I could do it, I leapt out of bed with such stealth, like a Japanese ninja. Swift and soundless, I moved across the polished floor with the only sound coming from my pounding heart. So far, so good. I managed to creep out the door. Not having seen the dark corridors and other hallways shooting off like a maze in many directions at night, the whole place felt bleak and uncertain. What if I escaped altogether? Would anyone even know I was gone? I tried to stay focused, to concentrate on the target of getting to the toilet and back to bed without detection or an unwarranted attack. The corridor was long and dark and on my left side there was a row of windows with each window veiled by a long chiffon curtain. As I scurried to the toilet a curtain must've been caught up by a sudden breeze. It billowed out at me, covering my face as I passed. Terrified, I was entangled in what looked like a ghost. I quickly unwrapped myself and ran. I looked behind me and saw the perpetrating window in the distance slightly ajar with the curtain billowing once again. My heart was thumping, but I stayed silent. I had passed the finish line of my obstacle course. I'd made it to the bathroom!

Once I completed my visit, I rushed back to the dorm never stopping to consider escaping again. Back in bed, I pulled the scratchy sheets and rough woollen blankets over my head and, finally, went to sleep.

Morning time came as another anxious, overwhelming activity. We'd all scamper to find clothes to wear and scrounge through the communal boxes of clothes. The bigger kids would use their power to push the smaller children away while they frantically scrambled for a piece of clothing. Often, I missed out, or just wasn't quick enough and was stuck with what was left, which was not always the most desirable attire. These pieces often had missing buttons or tears in the them. They really should've been in the mending box, if there were such a thing. Still, here they were hanging off me, making me self-conscious of my daggy and untidy appearance. The morning routine also included us unfortunates ensuring that all beds were made neatly before the bed monitor arrived. If sheets were wet, bedding was to be pulled off, ready for the routine parade. If beds were not made neatly there were dire consequences. It's not dissimilar to an army drill and, like all the other boys and girls, I stood at the end of my bed. This one time, I gazed back at my bed horrified to see something bulging from under the bed spread. I tried to pat it flat before the monitor got to me, but the bulge wouldn't budge.

One girl already had wet sheets and was crying as the

monitor reprimanded her. 'Stop being a sook,' she'd said, and then raised her hand and slapped her.

I was full of anxiety and fear waiting my turn at the end of the row of beds. I knew I couldn't fix the bump now; it was too late. Any false moves would draw attention to myself. I watched the monitor bounce a penny off another bed.

'Well done,' said the monitor. 'Down for breakfast you go.'

Finally, she reached my bed. She stood about five foot ten inches tall and had red long hair and a freckled complexion. She was the same age as my sister who was in the teenagers' dormitory, and her brother was a friend of one of my older brothers. She towered over me. Still I looked at her, hopeful she'd recognise me as the sibling of her brother's friend. She noticed the discrepancy in the bed, and then ran her hands over the offending sock or unruly blanket.

'There's a bump here,' she scowled.

I nodded, my head down.

'Do it properly tomorrow, or else.'

I looked up, hopeful. Maybe I wouldn't be slapped?

'Fix it now! Then head to breakfast.'

Relieved, I went down to the dining room. It was filled with children of all ages. If we had siblings, we were unable to be together, as it's not really allowed. I could see my two brothers, P8148 and P8147, at the boys' table. Then I noticed my older sister, M8136, sitting across from the bed monitors at the same table, chatting and eating breakfast. I felt too scared to make eye contact with her. I looked at my brother P8148 who smiled back at me. I was the youngest out of the four of us, and I realise now that I was victim to a situation that was completely out of our control.

I felt sad I was not able to be with my brothers and sisters like normal siblings. We weren't allowed to hang out or play together. Instead, we were to submit and obey the rules of the home. Only sometimes did the kind nun from the nursery, Sister Paul, allow us to spend time together, particularly when Sister Agnes was away on sabbatical. These were the best, when the routine changed and the sun shined in. Both of my brothers seemed to love spending time with me so much that sometimes they would fight over me.

'It's okay,' I'd say. 'I'll play a game with both of you, don't fight.'

My eldest brother was protective, and I loved it when he pushed me on the swing.

'Move your legs,' he'd yell.

'It's too high,' Peter cried.

'She loves the highness,' the eldest would reply. 'She can reach for the clouds.'

'Higher, higher,' I'd squeal.

Then I would beg them for a song.

'Oranges and lemons, says the bells of Saint Clements. You owe me a farthing, says the bells of Saint Martins.'

Those play times with my brothers would fill me up with a sense of happiness. I felt protected and wanted. There were moments there I actually felt part of a family; but then, as quick as those feelings flooded in, they'd be swept away by the actions of those holding the external strings of power over me.

Cherry red shoes

My first lesson in survival came in the form of a pair of cherry-red shoes. It all began when a few boxes of new clothes arrived, which had been donated by the likes of Myers and other department stores. For us poor unfortunates who had nothing, it felt like Christmas. To add to the excitement, there amongst the donations was a box of last season's shoes. That's when I fell in love with shoes, namely a pair of patent leather, cherry- red shoes. I'm unsure what I was thinking, only recalling the sudden desire for these shoes, and like a starving lion waiting for a morsel of steak, I pounced for them. But, before I even had a chance, they were snatched away from my grasp.

I remember obsessing over them, wanting just one chance to wear them, to look beautiful with my red shoes like Dorothy from the *Wizard of Oz*. Eventually, after putting far too much thought into their beauty, I devised a plan to achieve my dream and wear them, even if it were for only an hour. I decided I must have them. I was gripped with the idea of the shoes, and I lay awake until dawn formulating my plan. The plan was to be all dressed and organised before the wretched bed monitor came into the dormitory.

At dawn, while the other children were snoring, I leapt out of bed and ran to the box where I knew they lay. I picked them up. They were glorious, and I couldn't wait to slide them on my feet. Unlike Cinderella's glass slippers, I found them to be mostly a comfortable fit, regardless of being just a bit too tight. I quickly found clothes, dressed myself and then hopped back into bed, shoes and all. As planned, when it was time to get up, I was all dressed and ready for the bed monitor. I made my bed perfectly and when the bed monitor motioned for me to move along, I headed down to breakfast with my two feet squeezed into these shiny shoes. My feet were arched and tight, and I'm sure I was walking like a Chinese woman with her feet freshly bound, restrained. Still, I didn't care, even without room to wiggle my digits. No one was getting my shoes, well, not today. Then, when night fell, I hid my precious cargo under my pillow and simply squeezed my feet back into them in the morning. I remember showing them off to my elderly friends who lived in the rest-home wing of the home. They were delighted to see me in such beautiful shoes. I would play and prance around the garden like a swan, and for a moment, I felt special.

But, all good things must draw to a close, which was

the case with my cherry-red shoes. My feet really were too tight for the shoes and they began to blister. Of course, once those blisters burst open, I had to return my shoes back to the common box. I didn't care, I'd learnt to be tenacious and to not give in. That little pair of cherry-red shoes taught me how to survive and made me feel empowered. Even if it were only for a very short time, my soul soared, and I felt victorious. I can say this really was my first lesson on how to optimise many outcomes, a trait that's travelled well for me throughout my life, as some of my colleagues would attest to. In my profession, it's not easy to cut through red tape. There are many boxes to tick, regulations to fulfil, and obligations to meet; however, on regular occasions my colleagues often balk at how I've optimised best outcomes for the most vulnerable in our community. I seem to have a natural ability to gain outcomes for my clients, including unprecedented results that came because I didn't easily give up, especially when the going got tough. I've come to acknowledge and appreciate this trait, which I equate directly back to the tenacity I was forced to build while living in the orphanage.

Another rule we had to follow in the mornings included praying on our knees for rain, for sun, for the sick, for the dying, but never for ourselves or our plight. Our knees grew sore with callouses and pain after long periods of praying. The prayer routine went on every morning after breakfast.

It was called chapel time. Sister Elisabeth called it a time of reflection. Before we went to chapel our heads had to be covered with a scarf, and our hands were slipped into gloves. We would all kneel on the cold, wooden floor. I often felt restless and fidgety and would struggle to find any peace.

'Praise to our Lord Jesus Christ, Amen,' we'd repeat.

Praying for God's forgiveness seemed like a never-ending chore. I couldn't sit still, and I tried to stop twiddling the tip of my glove through the service. I often feared getting a belting for not paying attention, or looking to be fidgeting and not focusing on prayer. This one time I set my mind to staying still by gazing up at Jesus on the cross with his sad tormented face and the crown of thorns on his head, blood dripping down his face, nails in his hands and feet. I remember thinking, why must you suffer Jesus? I had heard that Christ had risen and that he would come again, but I wondered how he would free himself from those nails. I had a lot of unanswered questions. The statue of Mary reflected her as a serene and peaceful mother, nursing the baby Jesus. She seemed to love him so much. If that was so, why did God the Father have to give away his only son?

As soon as chapel finished, we'd go off to school, for myself pre-school. We'd leave our scarves and gloves in the basket outside the door, and then file into a line following oldest to youngest to return to the big building. Some of the older children were used for cheap labour and would do laundry for the big hotels, for which the church was paid. Every day was comparable to the next as the routine of the place stayed the same. The weekends were different for some children that were on the bad behaved list. They were lined up to receive a flogging. Dangers seemed to lurk everywhere, from nasty nuns full of bitterness and cruelty to damaged older kids who were always angry.

Sunshine On My Shoulders

Hair-wash day was a communal exercise at the orphanage, which, by the grace of God was a lot nicer than bath time. In fact, it was one of my favourite times. All the children would line up where the sun always warmed the east side of the building. Warm buckets of water and towels and soap were made ready for the volunteers from the local parishes who donated their time to wash our hair and do lice checks. They usually used the plain velvet soap provided, but sometimes one nice lady brought along her own shampoo. Usually, she would choose the little dark-haired girl with the big brown eyes, the smallest child sitting on the step staring at her while saying in her mind, please choose me, please! Everything about this lady was caring and tender. And when she spotted me on the step, I would wonder if she was reading my mind and picking up on my desire to be chosen by her.

I was more than happy to chat to this woman as I'd

remembered her from prior hair washing days. I'd wait patiently to see if she had her shampoo in her bag and was glad when she did. She was careful to conceal her bottle and when my hair was wet and tipped back, she'd rub a shilling's worth of shampoo from her palm into my hair, ever so gently. To this day, I remember the smell of that shampoo. It was like honey and berries and was a pink colour. As it foamed up, the lady would make a little set of ears from the white foamy mix. 'Now you truly are a possum,' she'd say.

Once all the washing was done, I'd gently rest my head back and she would rinse the solution out.

After that came the best part. As the dry towel was wrapped around my small head, the lady would caress my cheek. For a moment, all I would taste was the scent of hope as I breathed in the earthy smell of this lady and her scent of violets. As I looked at her smiling at me, I'd be inspired to smile back. Then, I'd sit in the warm sun waiting for my hair to dry, feeling for the shortest of time snuggled and nurtured. The feeling was tremendous, and I tried to hold on to it, along with joy, for as long as possible. It was all mine.

Comparatively, communal bath time was not one of my favourite times. It would include having to take off all my clothes and wait in line for another child to finish their 'quick' bath. Nothing was private. Bath time included standing naked in front of the other children waiting to get warm.

Everything was communal and it was dreadful. The nuns stood around and ordered you in and out. The water was used multiple times for three or four children, and there were five baths in total. Sister Agnes, with her sadistic manner, would monitor us, which usually ended in a bright red raised mark left from her hand on a wet back or buttocks. Back then, if I just stood next to water, I'd want to pee. I was not allowed to leave the line-up. I'd be on tenterhooks, jiggling there trying to keep warm knowing of my weak bladder, hoping to be the last one in the bath as often, by accident, I would wee in it.

This weakness left me prey to the brutality of Sister Agnes, who was aware of my condition. Sure enough, I would have an accident in the bath and while my body was wet. She would slap me so hard I'd wear a red hand mark. The violent connection of her hand with my legs, back, or bottom felt like the burn of a hot poker fresh out of a furnace. Looking back, it's astonishing how the imprint of her hand actually looked like a red rubber glove! It would remain there seared onto my back or legs as a stinging reminder of how alone and unloved I felt. Sadly, years later, in 2016, I found out that I have a kidney disease.

In fact, it was this that motivated me to begin the search of finding my biological father. When it came to the truth about him, many things were whispered about who he might be. Many assumptions were made. Apparently, my mother was seen with a man younger than herself. That does not mean he was my father. He was known as a standover merchant, a bully, not scared to lord it over a woman, known to be violent. Not that upstanding in the community. It remained like some dark secret, which, in my imagination, became a potentially worst-case scenario. Maybe Mum had no idea who my father was either, maybe she'd been in a self-medicated drunken state. Thankfully, genetic testing is a big part of our lives these more technologically advanced times, and regardless of all the theories in the world, DNA doesn't lie. Often the outcome doesn't make life-altering changes, but it can offer some connection to distant relatives, or family that are close by.

Although DNA cannot assist with the true, raw emotions of how one came to be, it can assist with clear scientific information, and I was willing to leave religion behind for a scientific answer. Years prior, science helped me pin the first piece of the puzzle together with my olive skin and dark brown eyes. My life was a challenge because I presented much darker than my other siblings. My experience was that in my own family, being illegitimate was not a great start. Adding to this were some issues about my darker olive skin. Further, as part of the Forgotten Australians, I was whisked away so young that I lost my identity and any chance of connecting culturally, or in any other way with either side of my parents' families.

During my pregnancy with Jessica, I was very unwell and required hospital admission. It was here I was visited by a haematologist who definitely felt there was Mediterranean background in my DNA. This afforded me my very first important hint at the age of twenty-two years old. I was extremely low on iron, and the haematologist told me I had thalassemia, a condition consistent mainly within Mediterranean bloodlines. Science to the rescue.

I didn't do anything with this genetic information, not for another three years. I was very sick, and my husband was also tested for thalassemia minor. If he had the condition too, it meant our babies could've had the major gene. This would've been dire as it often leads to death in babies. I remained curious, as I had a feeling there was an Italian connection in my bloodline somewhere. When I became pregnant with my third child, I confronted Mum and demanded she tell me who my father was, but she was mentally incapable of answering my questions. One day, I decided to follow up on a man's name that was whispered on the family grapevine as him being possibly my father. My dear friend, Justine, went to school with his son. He'd moved away to Melbourne, and through acquaintances, I located his number. I plucked up the courage to phone him. He turned out to be the most disdainful, ungentlemanly man I've ever encountered. He was rude and unsympathetic of the situation I found myself in. During the call, he flew into a defensive rage and after that I gave him what I considered a piece of my mind. Then

I ended the call abruptly. None of this seemed to make sense, especially because of my many dreams. I will talk about a spiritual connection to someone later. Still, I had only one lead at this time, so I held onto this one thread.

In 2016, I stumbled upon the same man's name in my ward files. His name was listed as knowing my mother. The possibility of being related and liking him were two very separate things. My health was now in question, memories from a previous phone call all those years ago had repelled me, but what if he was my biological father? I needed to know. My daughter drafted an email to this man's son. I was pleasantly surprised to find the son to be the complete opposite to his father. He was gentlemanly and extremely compassionate and intelligent. He indicated that he and his own mother's life had not been a dream. We eventually met together on a few occasions to exchange stories and see if anything matched up. There were small themes, but nothing palpable, excepting that his mother remembered his father attending court for something the year I was born. Was it possible? Was this angry man my father? His name was the only man's name listed in my ward file. We ordered a DNA test and my potential half-brother and I took the test to eliminate any further confusion. It eventually came back as no genetic link. The son indicated he was a little sad, as he thought it might be nice for his young child to have an aunty.

That was a lovely compliment coming from a stranger whom I'd only recently met. In some ways, I felt glad we weren't related, although, I still felt sure there was a definite Italian link because Mum had mentioned something in passing about an Italian grandmother. Nevertheless, he was not a match in any way at all. *Phew*, what a relief.

What was interesting, though, was that I discovered there was a direct link to the 'man' and an Italian family from the same town I was born in. This made sense, as I knew Mum wouldn't have travelled far. For most of my childhood and throughout other stages of my life, from teenager to adult, I've had vivid dreams of a grandmother who is warm and friendly. Usually, I would arrive at her house. She lives in an adjoining home, upstairs out the back. She is a very earthy lady with a no-fuss approach. In the dream, we are often together in her garden and then suddenly, she'll be gone, and I can't find her again. This dream has been with me throughout the vicissitudes of my life. The dream is always at her home, which varies from dream to dream, but it is usually attached to another home. More recently in the dreams, she's saying she lives up high. I don't know if the dead communicate, or, if our ancestral twine is so connected that we are reaching out to each other. It sounds totally bonkers, but it's completely true. I believe the grandmother is my father's mother, and she wants me to find my family.

The cocky with Tourette's

The orphanage sat on at least a twenty-acre estate. As I got older, I began to venture further outside my dormitory and the confines of the main buildings. These adventures mostly began around the front building because there was a beautiful garden there used for a dual purpose. The elderly people that lived in another section of the home would sit out in the sun before and after lunch. The orphanage children were discouraged from associating with them. The other purpose for the garden was to provide a façade to make the place look welcoming and caring. The garden housed a big palm tree in the middle, and there were plots of roses and lavender and other beautiful, scented shrubs. Sister Paula would sometimes take some of the preschool children for walks. We all had to hold hands and stick together. At the back of the home there was a good ten acres of free land. We were not allowed to roam the land. We always had to be accompanied by an adult, otherwise we were deemed to be out of bounds and trespassing on the groundskeeper's area of residence.

There were lots of cypress trees surrounding his property and I remember there being a very large, brown brick chimney close by on the property. One time, I was caught out of bounds and received a hefty beating for my curiosity. Within this free land, there were plenty of vegetable gardens, and alongside these, a large hen house. Inside it were many chickens and a rooster. When we went on walks with one of the nuns, we were allowed to help collect the eggs. There was also a large white pet cockatoo in a cage. He was called Cocky and belonged to one of the elderly residents.

'Why is he all the way down here?' one boy asked.

'His owner talks to him a few times a day,' commented Sister Paula in her Irish accent, who then assured us it was all okay and that every day he was fed a piece of apple or pear. She then went on to say that he'd been moved away from the front of the garden where the elderly ladies sat, because he initially belonged to a publican who ran a hotel, and he learnt too many naughty words. Just as she said that, Cocky began to screech. 'Shut up, shut up.' And then followed this up with something cute like, 'Dance, cocky, dance.'

The cockatoo resembled a bird with serious Tourette's. It had uncontrollable ticks and then screeched out curse words. Then, he would break into saying something cute like, 'Cocky like scratch, Cocky like scratch.'

We'd all laugh, making the bird became more animated with all the attention. He went on and on and on, 'Polly wants a cracker! Shut up!' And, a few other things.

'It's time to keep walking, children,' Sister Paula would say. 'His beak should be washed out with soap.'

'That's what Sister Agnes did to Danny boy,' I replied. 'She told him not to use God's name in vain, and shoved the soap right in his mouth, Sister.'

'Move along,' Sister Paula replied.

We did as we were told, but we could still hear Cocky. It made me smile and evoked the idea of a magic talking bird.

After a few years at the orphanage, I became familiar with most things: the staff, the children, the comings and goings of new arrivals and others leaving, the nuns (the ones who required a wide berth and the more approachable, friendly ones). Many times, we were left without supervision. One day, I was in the playground and one of the bigger boys took my hand and asked me to play with him, so I did. The boy then asked me to hide behind a log and lay down. I remember thinking it was a fun game, so I went along with what he asked. The boy started doing things to me that as a four-year-old I didn't understand, and when I wriggled and tried to get away, he hurt me. I could see Sister Paula in the distance coming towards the play area, which was a long way from the building, and when I pointed that she was coming, the boy pushed my face hard into the dirt and told me that if I yelled out, he would come and get me again and he would tell Sister Agnes that I was bad. As soon as I had the chance, I ran as fast as I could away from him with all the strength I could muster.

I wasn't going to trust any other older boys that easily again, but neither was I going to tell on him. I kept this secret locked inside a long time. In any case, it has taken me years to even acknowledge this happened or to talk about it. I do know veterans who served in the war and faced many atrocities and who've mentioned to me they found themselves shell shocked and disassociated because of the traumatic nature of their experiences. Perhaps, as a small child, that was the same method of detachment I employed. In a way, I'm grateful to these innate skills that subconsciously assisted to protect my small mind from permanent damage. When I think back, it makes me sad to realise that this older boy of around eight or nine years had clearly experienced some form of sexual abuse. I understand it is quite natural for children who are being sexualised to think it's normal behaviour, and do the same to others. It seems plausible, knowing what I've learnt over the course of my career in social work that the boy, through his behaviour, could've been reaching out for help in some way. When this happened, both of my brothers had already gone away. I missed them terribly. My life was lonely.

My eldest brother was the first to leave. I recall waving goodbye to him. About ten months later, my other brother went. When he left, he went with someone with the same name as him. A lot can happen in one hour. An hour could be life-altering. A child could be smacked, abused, shunned, lost, molested, locked under the stairs, be starving, or beaten by other children. Abuse can happen within seconds, and so quickly. In some ways, my brothers provided me with a sense of protection. They never did come back to the Sisters of Nazareth.

The garden

One of my favourite places in the orphanage grounds was the garden. Here, my tactile nature was provided with sensory overload. I felt free, and loved the smells and the colours of the garden. Initially, the children's home was organised, really, to house the aging population. Nazareth House sat on a very big acreage of land, and like most Catholic establishments, they were positioned well. I loved flowers, especially lavender and roses, camellias, daphne, boronia. Lavender remains my monument of love to the elderly women in my life, especially the ladies who once resided there in the old age home. One day, I came across the elderly ladies making lavender bags for the annual Easter fete. I thought this was heaven, the scent of those beautiful flowers. I remember rocking up to some Flo's door. I knocked, she opened and looked down at me. I'm sure she was extremely surprised to see cheeky me asking for her prized lavender bag.

Flo couldn't refuse and handed me one, and a few sweets.

I kept sneaking up there until she wasn't there anymore. I was always an old soul and all my life I've been attracted to keeping chickens and beekeeping. I attribute these loves as coming from my time dreaming in the gardens. I never understood why that boy had hurt me and for many years I thought I must've been bad. The weeks after that happened, I would pretend to head out to playground, and then I'd slip around the front of the building to get closer to the elderly ladies. After a while, I knew them all and they knew me. They were friendly towards me and they never once told me to leave. I'd watch them collecting lavender and then making the lavender bags for the fetes. I even joined in pulling the little purple flowers of sprigs of lavender. I was able to move freely. However, I'd always be cautious to ensure I wasn't caught by the nuns. I even went up to Flo's room to get the odd sweetie. I was given a lavender bag on my birthday. I suppose I'd told them how much I loved the smell so many times. I hid that little bag under my pillow in the day and sometimes took it if I wore a dress from the communal box with a pocket in it. Clothing with pockets became something to behold.

At night, I would squeeze my lavender bag to remind me of my old friends that sat in the garden. They were a godsend. The garden was my escape, my place of happiness. I felt safe there if I played alone because the elderly ladies often watched on. I loved playing with the slater bugs. I remember how I'd cover them over in the hope that they'd stay in once place, but they never would, for when I returned the next day to find my make-believe family of bugs, they'd always moved on. Sometimes, orphanage kids went on holidays. This one time, my sister, who was still in the children's home, had gone to her older sister's wedding. She was my sister too, well, half-sister, but I was not allowed to go, and when my sister returned from the wedding, she told me both my brothers had been there.

I was very sad to have not been included, but that's the way it was with Mum's side of the family. Nana would often travel down by train to visit the other three grandchildren in the home, but she had no interest in seeing me. I was the illegitimate one. Nana was good at averting her moral eyes and ears away from even the mention of my name. If my name was accidentally revealed, there was an unsaid silence. She consistently sabotaged me from spending holidays with Mum by blocking these opportunities. She would request to have my older sister and the boys. The older children were not to embrace their little sister. I suspect they had their own insecurities. If they upset Nana, she may not have visited them so much, so perhaps to avoid upsetting her, they made no real reference to me. I was more than invisible. I just did not exist.

The fact is, Nana, caught up in her Victorian principles,

had socially excluded me and, in the end, my half-siblings had to just go along with it to keep the peace. Children, by nature, are very inclusive until they learn how to exclude others. It's a form of social bullying that can be as detrimental to someone's mental health as actual verbal and physical bullying. Silent violence is excruciating. I didn't spend much time with my sister in the orphanage really. She was much older and there were rules around separating the older children from the younger. Besides, my sister was often fickle. Sometimes she might be irritable, short-tempered, and grumpy; other times she'd be helpful or caring by doing a nice thing like combing my hair. She would give me mixed signals and I was often unsure and weary of her. Still, I would persist, and I often hung around her until she told me to go away. But if she was happy to see me, I stayed. As I got older, I began to have a good grasp on her moods and movements. Still, I cherished her, and looked up to her. There was too much pressure for her to cope with, especially when dealing with her own sadness and traumas.

After my brothers left, she was the only sibling I had left to attach to. One night, when I wasn't well and couldn't sleep, I went to find my sister in the older girls' dormitory. Having risked being mauled by the demon dog, I asked if I could hop into her bed. Thankfully, she lifted back her scratchy blanket for me. I was desperate to tell her something, but my sister told me to shush, and be quiet. Eventually, we fell asleep. In the dark of the morning, we woke up and my sister pushed me out of bed. 'Quick,' she whispered, 'back to your bed.'

I ran quick and quietly back to my dormitory. In the morning, the bed monitor came in and she was quicker than usual having started on the opposite side. My bed was on the right, at the very end. Everyone else was getting the tick of approval and were heading down to breakfast. All was looking in my favour as the monitor seemed to be in a good mood. When she finally reached me, I smiled and was told to go down to breakfast. I started to head down the hall when all of a sudden, I felt this pain hit me to the ground. 'I heard you in with your sister last night,' the bed monitor spat. She then booted me repeatedly in the crotch. I was scared and curled myself into a small ball. 'Tell anyone and look out!' snarled the mean monitor. 'If I catch you in there again, I will hurt you more.'

Left crying and in pain, I felt a terrible throbbing between my legs. Finally, I went to the lavatory and found I was bleeding from my crotch. Not understanding what had just happened, the sight of blood freaked me out. The reason I say this is because I began to think I was safe with my sister; I began to think she might protect me. It was to no avail. It's like putting your trust in the wind. On another occasion, I remember going to my sister's dormitory at night again and wanting to sleep in her bed. She sent me straight back to my own, but that didn't stop the bed monitor from finding out and doling out my punishment the next morning. I never felt protected at all as a child, ever.

The mind is such a precious jewel. It has an incredible way of helping us out when we experience extreme trauma and abuse by repressing the memories and giving us creative solutions to help us cope with our immediate surroundings. I learnt to hide. I learnt to retreat like a mollusc under its safe shell. See, the mollusc shell isn't hard to penetrate, but the snail or the crab can retreat and hide when necessary. I learnt to be orphanage smart, to read people and my surroundings. I counted upon myself and myself only. I stayed under the radar. I became the dreamer, wondering around the gardens far from harm, dreaming, laying on my back, making pictures in the clouds, picking flowers, chasing birds, climbing trees, anything that would deliver me to anywhere other than where I was.

Daisy dress and picnic day

One day, the kids who had brothers at the boys' home were told we would go there the coming weekend. I was so excited when my older sister told me we were going by bus to see our brothers. In preparation, I had my eyes on a dress in the communal box of clothes. The morning we were to go on our visit, I tried to get up early and get the dress I spotted. Unfortunately, I missed out and instead grabbed a lemon-coloured dress with a little print of miniature yellow daisies. I popped my dress on and was nearly ready to go when I noticed my front button was missing. I wanted to fix my dress and feel tidy for my outing. It was then my sister grabbed my arm.

'We haven't got time,' she said. 'Come on.'

We hopped in the small ten-seater bus with the others. We were all looking forward to the picnic with our brothers. I'd never experienced a picnic before, and I was so excited to be seeing my brothers. As the bus pulled up at the home, everyone was happy. As we were exiting the bus, I saw other children's family members waiting next to a Christian Brother. He wore a long, straight, brown robe. Suddenly, I saw one of my brothers, the younger of the two. I became preoccupied with my missing button, so much so that as soon as I saw him, I told him my button was missing and I needed a pin. When I looked at his face, he was serious and grave.

My sister then said, 'Where is he? Where is he?'

Where was my big brother? Paul was trying to not be seen by the Christian Brother and he ushered us both away. Once out of the Christian Brother's sight, he started to tear up. He didn't take us to the picnic, but instead to where our other brother, Peter, was in the boys' dormitory. When we got there, Peter looked all battered and bruised, as if he'd been punched and kicked. We stood there, huddled and crying.

'Don't worry,' Paul said, and then, like an android robot boy, he went and found me a pin for my dress. That was the end of the picnic. More sadness, more trauma.

I was able to put all of the pieces of my brother's suffering together when I worked for an organisation initiated by the government to broker counselling for anyone who'd been in orphanages or foster homes in Victoria from the 1920s-1980s. Many stories had been told of the brutal acts against children in care and they began to come out of the Australian capital, Canberra. I heard them before the apology, during the apology, and after the apology for The Stolen Generations. What I learnt through all of this is that children and families that are deemed as socially low by race, colour, or finances are often just poor, which doesn't mean not loved. Often families, and the wider community, have no control over the Commonwealth's or State Government's removal of children. Once these laws were passed, nothing else mattered. Recently, I attended Aboriginal competency training. The facilitator was Third Generation Stolen, meaning she was also removed about the same time as myself. That's three generations of removal.

The pain I see that only one generation of removal has caused my own family has been unspeakable. To listen to this amazing Aboriginal lady, who was actually taken to my town of birth to be placed with adopted parents. I was taken from this town to be put into an orphanage. Ironic, really. We spoke, and we had an instant spiritual connection. It was like we both felt this invisible piece of string between us. I listened to her describe the severing of three generations of her family. This would've been indescribable. The heartache and loss are incomprehensible. I learnt much on this day. I have the deepest respect, a respect I've had even as a child.

In 2009, Kevin Rudd delivered 'The Apology for the Forgotten Australians and Former Child Migrants.' I was invited to Canberra to be part of the historic event. Keven

Rudd had previously addressed the 'Stolen Generations,' and to this day there is still racism, but at least he took the bull by the horns, as it was a hot potato and extremely controversial. Part of my journey to Australia's capital was made easier as it was all planned. I had my ticket sent to me and I headed to the airport alone. I was to show up at Qantas Australia by 10 am and check in with our support group. To my surprise there were young people all dressed in orange. It was like going on a tour with the (Bhagwan) the Rajneesh movement. They were clearly meant to be visible. Turns out, the government had employed hundreds of helpers for us care leavers and once we arrived in ACT, they all converged on us, swallowing us up in their river of orange, perhaps making up for the lack of connection we received at the orphanages. I'd been given a program of events and felt more settled with an idea of the proceedings. I was escorted to my hotel room by one of the orange people, and I felt a surge of excitement. Once I felt comfortable, I went down to the foyer and mingled with some other 'forgotten' ones. Many chatted about feeling the same anticipation as myself. In some ways, the orange people were a blessing. If you needed to know something, there was always someone to ask.

On the first day of the apology proceedings, I mainly kept quiet and observed. That evening, we were all to be welcomed and there was a special dinner planned in our honour. We all came together: the young, the old, the angry, the excited. We were all guided in by the orange people. There were many dignitaries organised and we had VIP guest speakers. I cannot remember them all, however, I recall Senator Jenny Macklin who was a Minister for Families. There were a few others, followed by Malcom Turnbull. His speech was the most compelling. It moved me, and I was a Labor voter. The empathy shown by this man was tremendous and his understanding of the topic was delicately delivered to all of us in the room. That night, my sleep was restless as I felt unsafe. I could hear two people who had clearly been drinking alcohol, and they were not happy. Self-medicating with drugs and alcohol is a pretty normal occurrence for many that have suffered trauma. Sadly, institutional life does not end after the orphanage gates. Some, only a few, get misplaced on their way and end up associating with the seedy side of life, including crime, which escalates quickly to prison, and sadly, they are reinstitutionalised and the whole process begins again. It becomes a familiar pattern.

I heard the swearing and trouble intensify not far from my room. Alcohol was being snuck in, even though there were rules. I left it up to the orange people employed by the then government to settle it down. I did not feel that safe, even with the demon dog outside my room having now turned into angry, disgruntled 'Care Leavers.' Emotions were high and I was again on my own.

The next day came, and we were ushered into buses again and taken to the historic grounds of parliament. I actually enjoyed looking around at the grounds of parliaments. It was interesting knowing there was a post office there and other amazing things to view. History is one of my loves. I love to learn new things and have an inquiring mind. I also enjoyed reading about and viewing the paintings of famous prime ministers. When it was time, we all moved in through the big doors into the great hall. The build-up to the apology matched the titanic size of this room. At this point, I felt suddenly alone and began to notice some mothers and daughters together. It was then I wished I'd requested to take my daughter.

As we queued for some time while filing in, I began chatting to a group of elderly men. These men were child migrants and had been shipped out all together from England. They were entering the great hall in the same fashion now, all together, with one now in a wheelchair. One of the men had been a member for the local shire in Mundaring in WA. As I had lived there one time, we chatted about their lives and talked about a book called, *A Fortunate Life* by A.B Facey; he also held a seat in the local shire of Mundaring.

His journey began in Maidstone, Victoria and then moved

onto Mundaring Hills of Perth, WA. The story was about a child's tough journey and his consequent outlook on life. Eventually, we were all seated in the great hall anticipating the roll out of the National Apology. Thought-provoking footage was shown on the big screens and all the dirty linen was aired for all to see and we all remembered something of the past. What a mix of emotions it was.

I listened and cried amongst the generalised sobbing. My foster dad had said, tongue in cheek, 'If you see Julia, say hello.' At some point, I needed to use the bathroom. I headed out the big doors. On the way back, I stood for a while, and then as I looked to my left, Julia Gillard was right there beside me.

'Hi, Julia,' I said. 'My father said to say, 'G'day.''

'Are you here supporting someone?' she asked me.

'Yes,' I replied. 'Me.'

I toddled off and sat back down and then we all got to go up to meet Mr Rudd. I was amazed at his white porcelain skin and hair to match. I met Malcom again and thanked him for the delicate delivery of his speech the night before. The emotions were running high, and others were breaking and there were many tears of loss and overwhelming sadness amongst the grieving for the lost years. Every television network and newspaper was covering the events of the day. I felt there was a stereotypical type portrayed via the media. They often zoomed in on the most vulnerable. It would be nice if they had a blanket effect and chatted to everyone from all backgrounds. I would waste no time in articulating how institutional life had impacted my life. Also, I would pose the question: How do you measure success? I was tired of the pigeon-holing of 'Care Leavers.' I think I've succeeded against all odds, as have many others. I was happy to say goodbye to the orange people and gather my thoughts a little.

After the apology, I made my way back to the hotel alone, collected my luggage and took a cab to the airport. Finally, I found some peace at the busy airport. On arrival home and for many weeks, maybe months, thereafter, I felt something very unnerving erupting within my psyche, my soul, and my mind. I needed time to process and digest all that had occurred during that brief time in Canberra. It made so many things resurface. Nothing went away. I acknowledged my pain and disappointment, my loss of family and significant others. The abuse of all children. I kept wondering about my brother Peter's suicide. He suicided in 1995. No compensation will ever bring my beautiful brother back. He managed to keep his life together for decades, and he was a loving and beautifully caring father, a good and helpful brother. He had a happy buoyant nature and was extremely witty, attractive, and intelligent. Suicide is for men often triggered by past traumas and feeling of being inadequate. My brother just wanted to enjoy his children, all of them together, without needing to choose who came first, or who was more important than the next. He wanted simplicity and peace.

There wasn't a cloud in the sky the day I found you, or the day you were buried. A song comes to mind for you, my beautiful brother. 'The Day You Went Away,' by Wendy Matthews. The saddest realisation was knowing how disempowered my mother had become as we had been caught up in a terrible system. We could not get out and she could not get in. The system made it impossible for her to initially reach me in my first long-term placement in care, which was just out of Ballarat at Sebastopol, Saint Joseph's Boys Home. I was in the nursery for infants. The rest of the institution was filled with vulnerable boys of all age groups.

Recently I took a drive to Ballarat out of curiosity only to realise it was impossible for her to of come to see me. She had no car, no money, and it is so far away from public transport now, let alone fifty-nine years ago. It would have been a three-hour train ride from Traralgon, followed by another two hours from Spencer Street station. Then she would have had an eight-mile round trip walk. That's a total of seven hours.

This made me, a sixty-year-old grown woman, cry. I had only worked out why she had entirely lost her mind completely in the end. One whole day traveling, Mum would have been traveling home in the dark, distressed.

The times, they are a changin'

By the late 1960s and 1970s, orphanage life was becoming different. There were fewer children, and thankfully, both Sister Xavier and the bed monitor, Patricia, had gone, never to be seen again. One day, as an adult, while viewing an art exhibition, the bed monitor's name popped up. Could she have become an artist? Maybe. Somewhere between those paint layers of beauty, she'd been just another victim of a heartless system. Perhaps her life at the orphanage was as awful as the rest of us and she too was a subject of her environment. She was angry, cruel, and hurt the smaller children. Irrespective of this, her size nine footprint was embedded in my mind. She'd enraged such a vicious and spiteful attack on my small, defenceless self.

On my sixth birthday, I received a red sand pit bucket and shovel with a red rake to match. Inside the bucket was a packet of coloured popcorn. I was told my mother had sent it for my birthday. I was perplexed. How could this could be true? I didn't even know I had a mother. I'd never seen her. Not even a photo. I couldn't even grasp the concept of having a mother, or what one felt like to me. The only framework I had was the statue of Our Lady Mary, Mother of Jesus, or Mother Superior, and neither were the example of what having a loving mother was like. To me, family was an experience of people being torn away, one after the other. Still, I liked my new bucket and spade and I would've liked to have kept it for longer.

I'd experienced using something similar while on a holiday with a family who took me with them to Mornington Peninsula. I remember we sang the Seekers' song 'Morningtown Ride' as we drove down to the bay. I loved the expression *all bound for Mornington* because it was the truth; that's where we were heading. Sadly, my holiday didn't last long as I had an outbreak of hives and was delivered back early to the orphanage. During this time, Sister Gabriel, who was often generous, came to me one day with her small black leather purse open. She only did this when there were fewer children to give pocket money to. That only happened when there were leftover kids who were not able to go on holidays. Besides my trip to Mornington, this was regularly me.

One day, Sister Gabriel said, 'We'll go to the shop and you

can buy a bag of sweets. The money is changing and we need to use up the last few coins in my purse.'

And, off we trod. We all headed out of the gates with Sister Gabriel and up to the milk bar. This was a big deal, because we barely left the fenced and gated area on foot. The rule was to only ever stay inside the grounds. On our way back from the milk bar, as I was enjoying a few sweets from a small paper bag, I noticed a dog running towards me. I froze, then screamed and ran. As I ran the dog ran after me. It wasn't black like the demon dog prowling our dormitory at night, but it didn't matter, it was all the same to me. The fear was too much. I scrambled to safety but fell and hit the pavement quite sure that this brown mongrel would tear me apart like I'd heard in Sister Xavier's stories.

'Get out of it!' yelled Sister Gabriel to the dog.

It did not grab me or rip me to pieces. Instead, it ran in the opposite direction as chased by the good nun. On the 16 July 1969, man landed on the moon. All the kids were looking up into the sky. The orphanage had a television and all the children and nuns gathered to watch the moon landing. I spent the next few days looking up into the sky, then at night up to the moon. The war in Vietnam was in full swing with young men facing conscription if their numbers came up to match the birth dates. Music was more emotive and descriptive. Things were changing and so was the deinstitutionalisation of orphanages and children's homes. The next stage for an orphan was to be farmed out to cottage homes and foster parents. The State was emptying out the children to begin a new model of care. The homes were expanding and the church would fill up the old dormitories with the elderly. Evidently, this would be another area for growth for the Catholic Church. Out with the young, in with the old.

During this time, I was visited by someone the nuns called my mother. She was with a small blonde girl, who was with my sister ,and another much older girl, who apparently was a sister I'd never met before. This would now be termed as a meet and greet situation. Then, one night, while I was watching *Skippy*, one of the nuns told me I was going home later that evening.

Surprised, I looked up. 'Pardon?' I replied.

'Home, child. With your mother.'

I was handed a tiny case with two dresses in it marked with my number, K8135.

My mother came to pick me up and she was with a man who turned out to be the husband of one of my older sisters. At the age of eight, I left the orphanage in the dark of night with two relatives who were complete strangers. The next chapter of my life was about to begin, and I wasn't all that confident it would be better than the last.

Part Two
Life With Mum

Grapes, vines, and bees

My mother was never mentioned to me at the orphanage, and when I returned home, I also found out I had three older sisters and one younger one, Salvation Jane. Apparently, my oldest sister was married a year after I was born. This was because she was pregnant, which was hard for her. In those days, these arrangements were called shotgun weddings, because the father had to be seen to be doing the right thing. My second eldest sister had her first child in 1965. Apparently, I'd been an aunty since the age of two. Living in the house already with Mum was Mary, and Salvation Jane. There was another older sister and her partner living in the house, temporarily, but they pretty much left not long after I arrived.

This couple had to have been supporting Mum, as they were the ones who helped her get things sorted with the authorities and most importantly, they planned to get my older sister out of the orphanage first. Then I followed months later. They fooled the authorities by pretending they would be supporting Mum with extra income and stability, as this would look good and help to get us out. This was a good plan, but not a sustainable one. Although, once we were both out of the orphanage and this couple left, they did their best, being only twenty plus. It was a big portfolio to pull off. I gather there was some direction from the matriarch to get my older sister out. The ruse was a success, and a few months later, they took the other sister with them to live closer to other full siblings and Nana. I was of no significance, only a by-product of the plan to get Mary out of the orphanage. I detected this while reading the records, and although it's sad, it does tie in with my memories of that time. At times, another older sister would show up at the house with her husband, as his parents lived in Dandenong. This sister would rush into the house while her husband sat in the car. She wouldn't even stop to have a cup of tea. When her husband got impatient, which was the norm, he'd sound the horn. This sister would suddenly make up some excuse as to why she had to leave, and she'd rush out the door as quick as she'd been blown in. It was both strange and funny. It became quite the normal routine, which I found weirdly comforting. I had to find a new normal, really. I'd gone from this reformed, type of military style orphanage life, lacking in love or affection, to a life that was emotionally similar. You cannot force that attachment on two strangers. Blood connection doesn't change a thing. Sadly for me, life felt uniform, chaotic and unstable.

Looking back at records, reading through the files from the State, I noticed that even though I'd been returned, I was still a ward of the state. Mum had not been given full guardianship. I also discovered this Dandenong rental cost Mum fourteen dollars a week, yet her pension was only seventeen dollars per week. It must've been a constant struggle for her to pay that large amount of rent. I also saw in the files, a letter addressed to the State from a social worker who was requesting the State allow my mother more money, as it was impossible for her to survive, or look after us, with only three dollars left over a week. The lack of action from Mum's only husband to divorce her led to the holdup for many years for her in receiving public housing. She remained ineligible for housing or the full pension until the New Pension Act was passed in 1973.

Living in a house was new to me and I remember paying attention to specific details about the property, things that were probably unimportant to most children. First, there was an outside toilet and most of the rooms had a fireplace in the corner of the room. It was a large, old home with high ceilings and windows that had to be wound out using a little winder. There was a grapevine growing outside on the carport, and I was fascinated with the small bunches of grapes growing so close to the house; the bees loved buzzing around them. Not long after getting out of the orphanage, Mum ended up in the Dandenong hospital across the road from our house, as she had a gynaecological condition. You'd think I'd be over the moon to be returned to Mum, yet I had no recollection of having a mother. She was literally a stranger to me.

Even though the house was adjacent to a state school, I had to attend a Catholic school. I guess Mum was concerned the State might step in again and take me back at any time. I started school possibly sometime in December, as I remember the warm weather, and Peter and Paul had returned from the boys' home for Christmas. I remember we were walking to midnight mass and I saw a dog. I was so scared, I stopped in the middle of a big road. It took lots of coaching to get me across. In those days, Midnight Mass was a big thing on Christmas Eve, and in the 1960s, 1970s, and 1980s, many families attended. My brothers were allowed out for a home visit on other occasions, and I remember this one time when my favourite brother, Paul, who was so gentle and caring, brought a tiny, live white mouse home. It had pink eyes and it was adorable. Years later, the movie Stewart little reminded me of the mouse. Somehow it jumped out of my brother's hand and took off somewhere, like the rodent was finally free. We took chase after it, looking high and low. For the life of us, we couldn't find the damn thing. When my brothers left to get the train back to Melbourne to the boys' home, I promised Paul I'd find it. I used to look everywhere for months for that little mouse!

More recently, I went past that old house. They'd rebuilt a newer brick home, but the old shed was still there. Driving up, the first thing that came into my head was the little, white mouse, and then the rush of emotion for my brother, Paul. He was full of innocence and had a kind heart. Then, I thought about my older brother, Peter, who seemed so cruel and angry back then. He was always teasing me, but I can understand now. They must've had a dreadful time in the boys' home.

I can relate. Most of the time, I had no idea where I was, either. I would orientate myself by memorising landmarks: the state school next door, the hospital across the road. The Catholic school was a long walk from home. Mum would often be out doing the odd cleaning job for a few extra bob, so Mary, when she lived with us, would take me to and from school. On a few occasions she didn't turn up to collect me. The first time I recall this happening was on one of those really hot days, and I had to navigate my way home alone. Here I was in the big world of Dandenong, which was never a small country town. It was an unfamiliar world and scary. There were dogs and things that I had no idea of. Up until now, I'd existed in a very gated, orderly world. Now I had bigger things to fear: cars, buses, unknown people, animals.

My life was so disorientated, and I already felt fearful being amongst a family I really didn't know at all. The only person I knew was Mary, who was just unpredictable and often temperamental. My only hope was to focus on the landmarks. I looked for anything familiar: a supermarket, a milk bar, a red post box, a garden, a cat sitting on a front veranda. Eventually, I made my way home from school, hot, sweaty, and alone with my heart pumping with fear. When I went inside the house, I found my sister was already home, showered and cooled from the warm summer heat. Mum said I'd done well finding my way back.

I guess I learnt quickly how to be independent in the real world. It was a time of feeling happy with myself, maybe a little bit empowered. One day I actually said to myself, 'Yes, kids are safe out here.' But then, I overheard Mum talking to the egg lady as they were viewing the newspaper. They were discussing a little boy who'd gone missing somewhere. He had on a fluffy jumper, cashmere wool. I looked at the photo of him, his innocent face with a few missing teeth. Eventually, they found him. He was dead and had met with foul play. As a child there was stories about other missing children. The Beaumont children, three of them, left for the beach and never returned. Like myself, young children were made responsible for other siblings. No, I didn't feel safe after hearing these stories. I knew then I had to be careful.

Mum had told me not talk to strangers or get in a car with a stranger, so I was always vigilant and watchful. This wisdom is something that's stayed with me. In fact, this alertness saved me many times as a teenager, and other times too. It's like my intuition was just innate within, and I would listen to it, always. In my role as a community services worker, I've listened to women that are possibly in situations of danger. When they tell me their stories, it's like the hairs on the back of my neck stand up. This feeling is akin to that gut feeling a woman gets before being attacked. That's the first sense of danger. My senses have always been on high alert. It's an instinct that comes in handy, helping me slip away from situations before they happen, and there have been many close calls. For me, listening to my intuition is an animal instinct, which I link to survival. Most women and girls who are about to be grabbed feel the hairs rise on the back of their arms, or neck. That is reason enough to move swiftly. Always listen to your gut instincts. It will never let you down.

Transitioning

Not long after being back with my Mum, I realised there was no emotional connection between us. I think going through a process of transitional time, introductions, short home stays, etc, would've suited my personality better in the handover between orphanage life and family life. This new home life didn't come with the nurture or emotional nourishment I desperately needed. These people were supposed to be my family, but I regularly found myself at sea in a home of strangers with nothing familiar other than a clean bed. At times, I felt seriously confused and humiliated by some of the things that occurred in the very early days, particularly being deloused, which included the burning of my belongings.

There was this big forty-gallon drum in the backyard. In those days people would burn their rubbish rather than go to the tip. This one day, one of my older sisters took a packet of Redhead matches and grabbed my things from my suitcase and lodged two dresses under her arm. I ran after her and yelled at her to give them back with a high, anxious tone of voice. Within a few seconds, petrol had been tipped on my clothes and my previous life, in a material sense, in the suitcase was changing shape as it became distorted in the hot flames.

This suitcase had stored two dresses that really had never belonged to me. I was familiar with them. I knew one of them was one of the nicest in the box. Many times, in the morning we would all scramble for the best pieces of clothing in the communal dormitory. This morning ritual was something like a scene from the big department store yearly sales, where women on the television loitering around the large doors, would run in as soon as the stores opened like crazed zombies grabbing and snatching, wrestling each other to the floor with some garment stretched to its limit between their clutched fingers. We were pretty much the same, scratching for some decent clothing in the communal boxes. It was very stressful.

Everything was gone, now.

I felt inferior and extremely distressed. Who were these people?

The second part of this distressing situation, something I've only ever told my therapist and a friend about, was being dipped in pesticide like a sheep. Due to having a very poor diet in the orphanage, I was emaciated because of the lack of nutrition and the poor quality of food I'd been brought up on. There was no fresh fruit or vegetables for us. We were fed scraps while the nuns feasted on the best of the swine! Turned out, I was riddled with hook worms. I had high fevers and was under nourished, very skinny, and I complained of itching down below. Consequently, I found myself bent over someone's knee, perhaps my mother's, with my head down to the ground while she picked out worms from my back passage with a hair pin. All I could hear was a running commentary from the onlookers above. I felt, and still to this day feel, humiliated. It was a terribly distressing situation. This was not a simple undertaking, like a basic ablution, washing of the face or cleaning out of the ears.

I was mortified, unable to move, frozen with fear from having been poked and prodded. Afterwards, my bottom was so sore, and I was scared to go to the toilet and use my bowels. I took to disappearing away in a big wardrobe. I was so scared to go to the outside toilet; it was an awful time. I just got so worried I couldn't go to the bathroom. What else might come out after all that poking and prodding? My toileting habits had suddenly become of interest to Mum. Anxiety can cause constipation, and I was in the thick of it, especially now that I was thrown in amongst strangers, even though we were related. Being related doesn't make a family. Love and nurture cultivate growth and a sense of connectivity. After being poked and prodded like that, I now had a growing feeling of dread and self-consciousness. I was terrified to go to the loo. Now my life was in reverse. I was able to be invisible in the orphanage, just another number. But now I was constantly under the microscope and being watched so closely was unnerving. Nothing felt sacred to me anymore, and nothing made sense.

I was stressed and overwhelmed. This was the first realisation I had that there would be no confidentiality in this new life. We all have things we get embarrassed or feel ashamed of. Bedwetting, wiping runny noses on a sleeve, getting caught picking your nose. No child wants to disappoint their family. This transition impacted me to the point of trauma. I was a small child used to a very regimental life, which suddenly changed. I was now being observed and viewed very closely. There was nothing about my life going undetected; after being just a number, barely noticeable, and at times, an unseen child, I felt doomed to disappoint these strangers. Looking back, getting medication from the chemist or apothecary would have been a way to confront this situation. My family was definitely uninformed, or their methods had been some primitive Irish ones. A clove of garlic and a glass of milk would have been more effective.

I was a kid, and being unfamiliar with these strange

people, I was petrified of stepping out of line. What were the rules? I'd often find myself unsure in this different world, and it wasn't long before I became more withdrawn. At the orphanage, I found myself knowing the routine of what to avoid and what to embrace. The children's home was always militant and clean. Kids scrubbed the floors. On leaving the children's home, there were no after-care programs, or following up. It was simply sink or swim. Many kids were just handed a suitcase, like I was, and left the children's home gates completely alone, with no plan. I'm grateful that at least I had a roof over my head.

My mother battled with me from day one. It was the most alienated relationship I'd known up until that point. Nothing came naturally. No love. No hugging. I was merely existing in another world. A world of words and language. I avoided conversation at the orphanage and never heard many conversations. Words came as direct orders. Go line up for bed. Bath time. Mealtime. Prayer time. Just conversing for conversation's sake was very strange to me. With Mum, these strange siblings had constant conversations and I would listen to them bantering on. Conversations became interesting to me. They caught my attention. It's not like I was a mute, but to hear people chatting to each other and then talk directly to me like I was there was both unsettling and intriguing.

Other than the clean house, nothing else was familiar.

My nights were still fearful and I'd wake with hot sweats. I didn't know it then, but I also had post-traumatic stress disorder from traumas encountered at the orphanage. I was trying to find some common ground, some stability. It felt near impossible. I was struggling with the transition and felt pretty much that I was full of germs. I felt like I'd come to an alternative planet, or the Moon. Who were these people? Where had the only life I'd ever known, gone?

From my experience, instant family doesn't make you feel instantly happy and secure. For me, it was very much the contrary. I think about people who consider being foster parents, because while it's commendable to be devoted to caring for a child, especially one who hasn't got anyone to care for them, giving that child an instant family doesn't automatically give them an instant sense of self.

Moving from place to place

We didn't stay too long in Dandenong. I can see why looking at the records. I don't know how Mum was paying the rent and keeping us fed and clothed. I suppose she kept us all afloat by taking menial jobs here and there. I know she cleaned for a few people, and by this time, there was only Salvation Jane and I living with Mum. All my older sisters were living their own lives and keeping in close proximity to Nana. Still, we had to move to Gippsland, which meant a new school for me. For the most part, I disliked school immensely as I always seemed to be the one picked on. We didn't have the nicest clothes or shoes or anything, and I never felt good enough with myself. Still, I was a strong, gutsy character, and this is one good trait learnt from those orphanage days. I often knew what I wanted and would become easily attached to ideas or visions of things. A dreamer to the point of being swept up in my ideals.

On one particular day, I got carried away by a nurse's

outfit that I spotted at my local school fete. We hadn't long been in Morwell, but I was still allowed to go to the fete and I was given a couple of bob to buy a cake or some toffees. I was going to make the purchase and come back home with the treats but instead, I became completely obsessed with the outfit and wanted to spend the money on that. It was a white pinny with a red cross and it had a little scarf that also had a medical cross on it. I disobeyed Mum and bought this instead of the sweets. When I arrived home, I got a belting and was sent back to the fete with the outfit and the job of asking for my money back. By this time, there were no cakes left, so we all missed out. How selfish of me. We left shortly thereafter. Mum obtained a housekeeping position looking after a dear old lady in Hernes-Oak. It was a brief stay, but this setting has always left its mark on my memory. Hernes-Oak was a tiny little town nestled between the Haunted Hills and the town of Yallourn, a little farming town. The area was extremely rural with lots of farming land and farm animals, mostly sheep, cattle, horses. I would have to walk to and from school, and sometimes I'd get so lost picking blackberries and eating them. I'd be actually happy to return home. Sometimes, I'd come home to freshly baked bread, which we ate with lashings of butter and homemade apricot jam. The house we lived in was pretty old and the loo was a real old dunny can out the back. You could simply open the door and just look out at the paddocks. I'd moo to the Jersey cows. The dunny-can man came once a week to empty the cans. Before that, most people added phenol, to mask the smells. With no town sewerage available in small rural communities like this one, we depended on the can man to get rid of our waste. I observed him as he skilfully swung that can up high, and rested it on his shoulder without spilling a drop. It would be then replaced with a clean one.

I enjoyed our trips to the local milk bar as you could get all the delicious sweets you wanted. Three lollies for one cent, or a big bag of sweets for ten cents. That was thirty units of lollies. A fifty-cent bag of lollies was so many lollies you would seriously be bilious. Like the Faye White song, there were bullets, mint leaves, musk sticks, chocolate freckles, liquorice, bananas, choo, choo bars, hard boiled lollies, bull's eyes, and gobstoppers. This little shop stocked lots of things; most importantly, the bags of lollies, or we'd pick out a few favourites which were wrapped up in a small white lolly bag. There was a bus that took us into the little picturesque town of Yallourn. We attended the little swimming pool a few times, and I remember the glorious gardens at the bus depot as the bus pulled up. This town had a very English feel to it. I believe this was because many English people came to live here, in particular, many engineers like my grandfather's brother, Bert. Many of them became charge engineers.

Today, Yallourn is all open cut and no longer exists. The whole place had brown coal under it and was clearly put on the map by Brown Coal and Australian Paper Mill. Yallourn was literally gobbled up by brown coal and over the years, I noticed the town slowly being consumed by greed. From Hernes Oak we moved to a caravan park. We were still in the Gippsland area, but the caravan park was on the opposite side of the Princess Highway. In those days, there weren't paid traffic controllers guiding school kids near crossings, nor were there lollypop ladies in bright colours, waving flags and assisting small children to cross the major intersections. Not one. I had to cross that highway to get to the school. Just a set of traffic lights and pure luck got me to school safely.

The caravan was small and we were practically sitting on each other. By this time, I'd already become obsessed with watching television, and we had a black and white set, thankfully. We had the bare necessities. We used the public washroom for ablutions, while Mum watched over us, and then we'd pee in a bucket at night. If we had no money to pay for electricity or gas, we'd be cold. Simple. To stay warm, we'd hop under the old comforter sets. They were thick quilts with matching pillows. The caravan was always cold. I could never get warm. It was probably winter, as I kept getting chilblains. They were a horrid ailment to deal with. Your toes become red and extremely itchy and uncomfortable. This drives the sufferer crazy. I was a year or more into civilian life and we had already moved four times. This in itself made me twitchy. I was already prone to fidgeting and restlessness. I had too many allergies and they drove me nuts. After dinner, I remember pretending to be asleep, but secretly I would watch adult televisions shows. *Hawaii Five 0. In the Valley of the Dolls.* When I think of my mother, I see her as the adult, but somewhat failing to manage her life, let alone ours. She was possibly too unwell and, understanding trauma as I do now, I believe she was still locked away in her eighteen-year-old self somewhere. I am not a psychologist. I feel my mother just never matured. It was like she was stunted emotionally somewhere. She was not like the other mothers I eventually got to know. This made her and us significantly susceptible to being in the wrong situations or places.

I shouldn't have been watching, but my confidence was building. There's one thing I'll always remember about growing up in Gippsland, which is the freezing cold winter mornings. They'd be so cold that if the washing was left on the clothesline overnight it would be stiff as a board by morning. The visual of it snapping and breaking in half was often a figment of my active imagination.

Mr Bridgewood

Mum was doing her best, and I can see now she was trying to give us some stability. The boys were still at the boys' home, Saint Vincent's, and Mum wanted them out of there. Her plan was ongoing, like a working document. Get us settled, get the boys out. After housekeeping for the elderly lady, Mum answered an advertisement in a local paper for a new housekeep position. This second job wasn't as nice as the one she'd had in Hernes-Oak. It was rather a scary nightmare for us all, actually. This man, Mr Bridgewood, had been living alone for some time since the sudden death of his wife. He seemed incredibly strange, and it was Mum's job to wash his soiled underpants. I remember Mum trying to soak them.

To add to the nightmare, we all lived in the house. Not long after moving in, Mum accidently tripped upon a mat in the kitchen and, without realising, stumbled upon a burn mark resembling the shape of a body. Apparently, Mr

Bridgewood's wife's clothes had caught fire while she was cooking. The story goes that she later died in hospital.

Clearly, something had triggered Mum's anxiety, possibly the burn mark, or just him. He was super creepy. I remember having whooping cough, which is a very serious illness. For weeks I lay sweating in bed. I was very unwell, delirious with high fevers and completely zoned out in bed for weeks. Mum was stressed that Mr Bridgewood might do something to us. At night she used to put a chair against the door to keep us safe. She was terribly worried for our safety. From what I understand, once I was better, she answered an advertisement in the local newspaper. Des and Joe, two strong helpers, came with a truck. Within three hours, they'd moved us out of that kooky house while Bridgewood was at work. It is called a moonlight flit, only we took off in the morning. I had to change schools as we'd moved to Trafalgar. I feel proud of Mum, now. She didn't waste any time finding us a new house to move into. She must've saved up money to pay the movers and, I understand, she was trying to find us some stability. How difficult it must've been with her unstable mental health.

Mum remained friends with Des and Joe even though both of them were younger than her. They were nice men who didn't come from a drinking lifestyle. Joe actually went off to seminary and became a Catholic priest. As Des grew older he'd always pop by with his girlfriends. They were very friendly and decent people. I never felt threatened or worried when either one visited. I can confidently say that the situation at Mr Bridgewood's house was possibly the start of Mum's mental health relapse. Because after this move, I noticed how she became more agitated and violent towards me. Our relationship was pretty much on a downhill spiral, and I can only assume this was because we'd never bonded. She became very anxious and began to self-medicate. Also, she'd started to pluck out her hair, strand by strand. This is an anxiety illness called trichotillomania. Mum's mental health had become so very challenging. To this day, I remain grateful we escaped from that macabre situation, and to Des and Joe for helping move us.

Near deaths

In Trafalgar, I had a near death experience due to an Allen's Confectionary truck. It makes me laugh now as I look at these things from behind adult eyes. It's much less raw now than it was in reality. Maybe you could count Mum's attempts to terminate me as near-death experiences. Because of my quirky way, I actually chuckled while writing this, so understand my sense of humour is with me, always. I see so much through a smile. Humour makes me a better person and gets me through things much easier. If you watched the *Benjamin Button* movie, there is this repeated skit where this elderly man in the nursing home keeps telling Benjamin about his near-death experience by lightning. It's so funny. Throughout the movie there are visuals of the elderly man being zapped, and then there are these short snippets of the different incidents of being struck with lightning. It reminded me of my young life.

In this house, Mum was mentally in an okay space. She

seemed to be managing her triggers far better now that we were living in a quieter rural area. I found going into any bushland or watching television my second love. It was a great escape from some of the issues I faced as a child. These forms of distraction or disconnection were extremely helpful for my malleable and developing mind. In those days, our milk was delivered by the milkman every night. You'd hear the trotting of the two big Clydesdale horses, and I loved watching them appear down Waterloo Road. There was some simplicity in life back then. The baker delivered bread, as well. This one night, I was enthralled in watching one of my favourite T.V shows, *Batman*. The show was just at the stage where Adam West (Batman) and Boy Wonder were in the middle of the POW, WHAM, BAM, action of smash fighting.

Mum asked me to take out the milk bottles and they would leave the milk in the crate outside. The crate sat near the letter box at the front of the gate. I hesitated, as it was only minutes until the Joker and his crew would be cleaned up by the dynamic duo. Then, just as I headed out the back door, there was this mighty crash. An Allen's confectionary truck suddenly came smashing through the front window of our house hitting a couple of chairs. It drove clear over the gate and post box where I should've set down the milk bottles in the crate. Apparently, the driver of the truck had an epileptic seizure. The ambulance took its time to arrive, and the man told mum and the neighbours how he hadn't had an episode for years. He was worried his condition might cost him his job. I felt sad for him but happy for myself when Mum complimented me. She was glad I'd disobeyed her. I loved Batman so much more after this day. Still, a bag or two of Allen's lollies would have been appreciated by myself at the time. I love sweets.

The stone angel

From this house, we moved to a unit at the back of an Italian lady's house. It was small with a sunroom to the side door. We cohabited with some younger people on the other side. The neighbours had three children and a black German shepherd called Jet. He was jet black with grey around his mouth. I was fearful of dogs, and black dogs were even scarier, due to the stories we were told in the kids' home. Whenever I played with the kids next door, I used to observe Jet watching us. He'd wag his tail and let the kids dress him up in frocks and hats! I learnt he was a gentle old bear and my trust slowly built. I'd started to learn to pat him and touch him on his back and face. One day, while we were all playing on a picnic blanket outside in the sunshine, I took my affection for Jet too far. I gave him a strong squeeze, much like a tight cuddle, and he nipped me near my right eye. On reflection, poor old Jet the German Shepherd possibly had arthritis. I had no understanding of animals; they still scare me. When Mum noticed, I told her it was my fault. No way did I want Jet to get in any trouble. He wasn't a toy, he was a dog, and I knew he was a gentle dog and liked me as he always wagged his tail and licked my hands. My love of dogs started with Jet and it's still with me today with my little Bob and our symbiotic relationship. He follows me everywhere. I adore him. Dogs are such loyal animals. My love doesn't stop there. My cat is always lazing around somewhere warm and comfortable. Then there is my love of chickens. I have kept chickens for over forty years. These days, Peking Bantams. They are super cute. Jet was my first four-legged friend, even though he was not mine. I would call him a rescue dog. He rescued me.

After a good year in this new area, I was becoming familiar with my surroundings. I had to walk along a long road to get to my Catholic school, but I didn't mind anymore. It made me feel grown up. I happily walked to school and made up songs on the way, and then would perform them in front of the class for show and tell when my teacher let me. I even skipped to church at times, as I could hear the bell ring on a Sunday. This was a time of growth. Along the path to school was a stonemason's workshop. I could hear the Italian mason speaking to his son in Italian while they worked in the yard. Their creations were truly fascinating to watch being made. Sometimes, I'd briefly see the beginning of a stone block being shaped and then the finished product a few days later would be on display. These were tombstones and crosses with gold leaf writing etched into beautiful gravestones. There were also magnificent statues, all white. The one I truly loved was a serene white angel. She must've been an order that was never collected, or perhaps the stonemason couldn't bear to give the angel up. This angel watched me go to school, and then again when I passed by on my way home. She made me feel safe, and I felt connected to her in some way, as if she were watching over me.

Many decades later, on a visit to Italy, I found myself in awe of Michelangelo's *Pieta* while visiting the papal city and entering Saint Peter Basilica in Rome. I was in awe with the way the sculptor etched into the marble, the depiction of pain in the Blessed Virgin Mary as she held her dead son, Jesus, in her arms and looked down with such agonising pain. The level of detail is unbelievable. I spent a good thirty minutes admiring this beautiful piece. It was truly thought-provoking and bewildering. My love of sculpture and the arts started with the Italian mason's stone angel. The *Pieta* has always stayed with me, as has the statue of David. I've always felt a strong connection to Italy. Could it be something to do with my biological father? Or, was it me simply holding on to wishful thinking and that one passing comment from Mum about my having an Italian grandmother? Some days, I wished that were so, and that I knew her and that the broken link in the chain of my lineage would become solid. When I uncovered a man's name in my ward files, I'd hoped the search for my father would be a simple link the dots, but it turned out that my life was never meant to be that easy. I applied for my ward files a second time. Often, this can turn up different news. There it was, I don't know why that man's name was even on the next lot of paperwork I had applied for. Ward files are like this every time you apply for your files. You might find additional information. I would say the policewoman, or one of the older girls said it, as why should their own father be responsible for additional children, especially because they were never his? This I understood completely. So, perhaps he was the only obvious choice. Clearly, I didn't know everything. My close friend knew both the father, and his son. She was instrumental in giving me an email as a contact. Then a new journey to rule in or out a biological link. DNA may possibly assist with clarity around my kidney disease. My daughter wrote an informed email to his son. He turned out to be a lovely man. We met up a few times and formed a nice rapport. During my conversations with him, we spoke about the Italian bloodline. He clearly confirmed there was no Italian bloodline in his family; this was the very first important clue. We received our DNA result, and we were not at all related.

DNA search engines are turning up all matter of elating

and disturbing evidential data. They are now becoming affordable and accessible for most who need to connect the dots. Some of the information can be very unsavoury.

For myself, my own lineage and origins were starting to surface. A familiar name was popping up spelt differently. It was an Italian name and there was one letter that was different from one I had known for decades. Then my answer came when a new person appeared on the DNA search, so I emailed her and introduced myself. I asked was there any family in Australia pinpointing the exact place I was born, and she said yes. The confusion came from my maternal grandmother's side and my paternal grandfather's side. They both went to America along with so many other relatives that made a beeline to them. Then I finally had the answer I needed; a man that had lived close to the town where I was born. And there it was. At fifty-six years of age, the journey had come full circle. She explained that one letter had been changed on entering the USA: her grandfather's, my biological father's uncle. He entered the United States after the Second World War. He had fought in the Great War with my biological grandfather (Nonno). The two brothers fought together alongside the American army. They both returned to Calabria in Italy and my grandfather died of an unknown illness in 1938. He was very young and left a young wife and seven children behind. One of the children was just a baby, six months old.

My own father was only three years old when his father died. Like myself, he grew up without a dad. His uncle had immigrated to America before 1938. Serving in the war gave him easy access and it was much easier to emigrate to the States. It was then that the 'd' was changed to a 'l' and instead of Tripodi, it became Tripoli. One letter can erase thousands of years of ancestral twine if it is left this way. There might be more to the name change. To complicate life a little more on my father's mother's side, there were other relatives that had also gone to America.

That was the direct connection to the two girls I had become acquainted with. Their nonna was the sister to my biological grandmother (Nonna Rosa). The search engine became a big fishing net with all these links. I had no one to navigate me to anyone, until this one lady gave me a name, a name I actually knew!

Logistics. I had seen a truck or trucks bearing this name. Trucks that had passed me on the highway to and from Gippsland over the years. Whenever I saw them, I always felt this strong connection, which at the time I shook off as nothing, just a weird feeling. Isn't it funny how life catches up with us?

It's as if no stone is unturned and nothing is left unused; it's as if I was meant to always see those trucks and to always have those memories. Did you know, most people don't realise they have kidney failure until they have less than five per cent of kidney function left? I stumbled upon my kidney disease while preparing for surgery in 2016.

Around the same time, I had become a member of ancestry. com. Part of the new search in genealogy was I had rendered my DNA sample and that's when a 'Calabrian connection' started to surface. This was an introduction to two-third cousins from America, Debbie and Robin. After lots of emails and conversation, there was still no answer, no new information. Still, it was thrilling to have a genetic link to them, and from all over the world. It took some time, but eventually I found a connection back to the town where I was born, in Gippsland. All it took was one email to the right person, ancestry.com, and three years of emails to many people, some happy to give me a small morsel of updated information. My daughter, who has the best investigative skills, actually had known one of her cousins, but we did not know we were related at the time. She had worked with a lovely lady with the same name and then she said I found a connection between you and them, and she remembered they had been fundraising for the Red Kidney Bus.

This bus is amazing. It travels around helping patients

suffering and needing kidney dialysis. It can travel anywhere. They had done a tremendous job building awareness about the need for such a fantastic medical resource. The big Red Kidney buses can be seen everywhere helping sufferers to manage a silent disease.

The puzzle was staring to come together. We were getting close. There was a problem. There were four brothers and a sister that had come to this very same country town where I was born, along with others that migrated between the 1950s through to the 1960s. We are talking hundreds of this family with the same name. My two-third cousins in America kept encouraging me to keep on my path to self-discovery.

Secrets

Who am I? I've continually asked myself this over the past fifty-six years. Within the traditional family, no matter how unusual or fractured, there is always that one person to measure yourself against. One person who might take an interest in you or the things you like. I think having role models and people in your life who champion you is incredibly important, more so for those of us who never had that grandparent, parent, aunty, uncle, cousin, or any loving older sibling or person, really, who genuinely cared for our emotional wellbeing or direction. To not have an advocate leaves a child floundering, in my opinion. Most of my childhood was spent trying to gauge danger or keep out of the nuns' or Mum's way by staying under the radar. For myself, there was no happy, no friendly, no *one* consistent person who cared.

This has left an unfillable gap, and as much as I don't want to be disappointed, a part of me hoped that my biological father would fill this space. However, I realise that people who you think or expect to fill those gaps often don't. When no love came from my home-life, I suppose I went looking for it at school, anything really, any kind of caring or emotion from a teacher or my peers. I often found Catholic school to be a contradiction. We'd be taught about the kindness of God, and then I'd be continually teased by my peers like I was some overall misfit. I would be called 'guinea pig,' and it was truly the nastiest attack, particularly for someone in my situation, a growing girl, desperate to be loved. If I had a bad day, I would run home quickly, just in case one of the older kids followed to taunt me more. I'd often pray to the stone angel many times while passing or running by.

I was often very unwell during this time of my childhood. In the winter months, I'd get terribly ill with whooping cough or tonsillitis. In summer, it was the dreaded hives, or haemorrhaging from the nose with blood. I always had this awful nervous energy and felt anxious, especially if Mum was a little out of sorts. One night after rushing home, I found a strange man sitting with Mum. This was the first time I remember seeing a strange man around the house. They were drinking beer and wine. And, would you believe it, he was selling vacuum cleaners! When I arrived, he instantly made a remark about me, saying, 'She's a cutie. This one's very dark. Maybe some wog in her.' He smirked, and then turned to his drink. After a sandwich, my little sister and I were put to bed. My little sister slept with my mother, as always, and I slept beside the wall in the same room as them. As the night went on, I could hear Mum become really drunk. My sister had already fallen asleep, but I'd started to cry. I was hungry. Mum had often threatened me that if I didn't shut up, she'd put a hot potato in my mouth. And on this occasion she was true to her word, although a hot potato wasn't her food of choice. She came in the bedroom this night with an orange, which she screwed into my mouth with such hatred and force that some of my small teeth actually snapped and broke off. I was in pain and left crying silently, too scared to make any noise. Suddenly, I heard a big bang, so I opened the door and Mum was on the floor, vomiting. 'Go away, leave!' I shouted to the man.

He hung around and just would not listen. Instead, he brought Mum into the room where we slept in one bedroom. My sister was in her normal sleeping place in the double bed with mum. I was in a camp bed on the opposite side of the room against the wall. He proceeded to undress her. At this point I was so distressed I was beside myself and ran straight out the door to the house next door where Jet the dog lived. He started to bark as I needed help. I was hysterically crying as I banged on the door. 'Please help us,' I pleaded as the neighbour tried to consul me.

The neighbour gave me a striped blanket to keep me warm.

I was wearing a shorty nightie set, and it had become cold. I was in some kind of shock. The lady wrapped the little soft blanket around my tiny frame. 'Call the police, now,' she said to her husband. I ran home and found the man undressing my mother, my little sister fast asleep in bed, and so I grabbed a broom and started beating him with it. 'Get out, get out,' I shouted. Jet kept barking outside. Finally, the police arrived. They came into the house and saw my mother's naked body and laughed. I will never forget those two useless policemen; it was such a male-dominated world in the early 1970s.

All I wanted was to feel safe for us and to be safe. This was out of control and in many ways out of character. I was worried for my little sister. 'You'd better leave, mate,' one policeman said to the man. Thankfully, he did. When he left, I locked the door. I kept a watchful eye on Mum. She kept vomiting, so I got a bucket for her and washed her face when she was finished.

The next day, I got up out of bed and washed my face like a mechanical robot. I was zoned out. I got dressed, wiped the smeared blood from my face, and went to school.

After arriving at school, I clearly wasn't coping. I sat under my desk, hiding my missing front teeth and the bruising around my mouth. During playtime I was allowed to stay in. I sat squatted under my desk. I was traumatised, exhausted, and consequently did not like school. I had nowhere else to go. This was it. The only place I felt safe was under a wooden desk. Teachers in those days, especially a very young teacher who had just come from Catholic teachers' college, would not have been equipped to deal with a situation like this one. I couldn't eat anything or drink, so I just sipped water. I dawdled home after school. When I approached the stone angel, I looked up at her. No answers still. Same old, same old. I kicked a stone on the path and with my head down, I kept walking.

When I got home, the man was there again, sitting in our kitchen, not drunk, but possibly trying to recompense for his abhorrent behaviour. He tried to give me some money. I wouldn't accept and walked away in disgust. I hid in the bedroom under my camp bed, worried there might be a replay of the previous night, but he left soon after I vanished. I was not even nine years old, but we had been moving from place to place.

My mother kept me out of school for the rest of the week. I guess the bruising was pretty noticeable. I was fine. I felt okay and everything was calm for a while. I just stayed out of her way and talked to old Jet next door. He sat there looking at me and licked my hand or nudged me to pat him again. When I got to school the following Monday, this lovely teacher told me to have a look in my desk. When I lifted the lid, I found my books all wrapped in yellow crepe paper. What a kind thing to do. I've never forgotten that small kindness shown to me when my life was like living in an obstacle course.

This was unlike the orphanage. There, you learnt to gauge and avoid danger. Life with Mum was unpredictable. I had no idea of the game plan and her random, unprovoked attacks. I never told my mother about the police being called. She was asleep. If I'd told, I would've been a goner! It was easier to act dumb and pretend I had no idea. That was the ticket.

These awful events of losing teeth and the other events of that night left me very bewildered and ashamed. I put it behind me, as always.

Plus, I had this need for approval. I wanted Mum to love me. I tried to never disappoint her. But, most days it felt like I continually did that by just being alive. As an adult, I had to forgive much and many so as to be my buoyant self. Forgiveness is better for me than becoming bitter and totally damaged. I have a very stable life. I know now that I am free.

Smokey

It's funny how you remember some things. I believe it must've been spring on this particular day, as the mornings were getting warmer. There were blossoms lining the road, which looked beautiful, laden with the soft pink and white petals. From the onset, my walk to school was not unlike any other until I met a grey cat under a bridge. He was an elderly cat, and I wasn't sure if he was dumped or had pet dementia or was just plain lost. I was worried he would get flattened under a car, so I tried to lead him to my home. Surprisingly, he followed me. I called him Smokey. As soon as he was out of danger, I ran back to school.

By the time I got home after school, I half expected him to be gone, but instead Mum said he must've been very hungry as he'd caught three mice! I was so happy as this pleased my mother. She'd been complaining about mice at the time. She liked him, so he was permitted to stay. I loved that cat, but my allergies didn't. I sneezed and wheezed for a good week. It was a constant battle, including coming out with the odd rash. Still, Smokey was the most love I'd ever had, so I put up with it. He was so warm and loving and was my first own real furry friend. He loved me and repeatedly showed me affection. It's hard to imagine how desperately unloved I was. Mum was never affectionate towards me. In fact, she was so removed from me emotionally that I truly had no understanding of what love was. At some of the worst times, I hid around behind the shed with old Smokey.

I celebrated Smokey as my sweet, old friend. Everywhere I went in the backyard, Smokey followed. I'd found love in a grey tabby tomcat. He smooched, he purred, and we became best friends. I used to tell him he was a gift from heaven above. I sang him songs as we sat out in the sun together. He liked Tom Jones' *What's New, Pussycat.* He seemed to like the big purple Agapanthus plant, with its foliage that looped over like an umbrella. It shaded him in the warm summer sun. In summer, the flowers were like long, tall sticks with sprays of purple flowers. Smokey would hide amongst them, giving him the advantage when peering out at the unknowing birds to see if he could creep in for the kill.

He was too old and too slow. Then, as autumn cooled and the frost came in, old Smokey disappeared. I looked high and low. I cried and wondered if my mother had taken him away as punishment. One day, I found him curled up under the Agapanthus bush, his favourite spot. He had died, and must've been there a week before we found him.

What a day

Increasingly, I felt my life was again in the hands of another. Life was continually unpredictable. Smokey had died. My home life was difficult. Catholic school was a constant struggle. I always looked daggy with socks that had no elastic so they just hung down, and shoes that were boy's school shoes. One day, I actually paid a girl a few bob to wear her shoes during play time so I could feel temporarily nice. I now see where my shoe fetish crept in. (No. I was never going to be an Imelda Marcos at all, especially as an adult!) Frankly, I hated myself; although, it's funny how life happens with its ebbs and flows, because just at this low point a few nourishing crumbs fell from the table. I was to make my first communion, even though I was older than the other kids making theirs. This was the third holy sacrament to be made; the first was baptism; the second was confession; and the third was communion. I would be presented in white like a little bride with veil and all. I would then have to go through a full requiem mass. After this, there would be a big table full of lovely cakes and bottles of coloured soft drink.

For some weeks, the anticipation of this event filled me with distraction. The day of my communion would be the best few hours of my childhood life. Besides, this would be the first time my sister had to sit back. This was my special time. I felt like Cinderella at the ball. The actual day started off a little stressful. I think it was because I had so much self-doubt and I didn't feel pretty enough, what with my bowl haircut and crooked fringe. Something inside of me just didn't feel quite right. My white dress was too big. It was a loan off a teenage friend, Cathy. She'd lived across the road from us on Elizabeth Street. She was a nice girl and was often at our home. She was a fringe dweller who didn't fit in much, either. Her mother was an alcoholic and she'd had numerous live-in creepy boyfriends. Sadly, one of these disgusting men got too close to salvation. I can only imagine how tough Cathy's life was. She said she had a knife keeping her door jarred shut, as her mother was continually passed out blind drunk leaving her to protect herself from the level five clingers. Eventually, the department stepped in and removed her. It was possibly too late. Still, Mum made her welcome in our house. She was embracing like that. I liked that about her, and I liked Cathy too. So, she brought the dress over and she also had a Kodak Pocket Instamatic camera.

I was made to be the model and pose while Cathy took a few snapshots. For this brief moment, I was the centre of attention. Me! Embracing the look of a small bride with a white veil and gloves. This was a moment to embrace, as moments like this one were not really part of my life. I remember the moment when the group photograph was taken. I was more concerned about my skinny legs. I was as skinny as a string bean, more self-conscious of my appearance than smiling. After the photos, we went to the school hall. My eyes lit up like Luna Park. It really was all I'd anticipated.

A table was full of little lovely coloured drink bottles with every imaginable flavour: lime, pineapple, raspberry, orange, cola, lemonade, creamy soda. And that was just the drinks! Other tables were covered with beautiful tablecloths and a spread of the most delicious party food laid out. There were things I'd only ever dreamed of, like fairy bread covered in hundreds and thousands of sprinkles, and the most divine cupcakes with pretty icing. The walls of the hall were adorned with buntings and colourful decorations. For the very first time, I was the invited guest. This was my very first celebration, ever!! I felt so included. I received this lovely little gold pin with a beautiful dove on it, and to this day, I've kept it. How? I do not know. But, I do have it and somehow I even have a photograph of the day.

What a wonderful feeling of excitement it was, as I sat with all of the kids who chatted and were talkative and ecstatic. Not as much as I was, though. This was a first! I remember looking across at Mum and my little sister, thinking this was my own special thing. No one was going to take it away. When I think back on that hour of my life, it was truly momentous and joyful. Empowering. Here, I was just being a kid, not a carer for Mum, or my sister. It was like all of the angels were singing a victorious song as I sat there feeling included. I froze this picture in my mind's eye for what seemed like a long time, before I was tapped on the shoulder and reminded it was okay to eat and enjoy. Me! The girl who was treated as an outsider most days with my sloppy socks and who paid to wear another girl's shoes, the girl who simply wanted to feel proud of her clothing and uniform just like anyone else but barely had the opportunity due to changing schools so often. Mum couldn't afford to be always buying new uniforms and sometimes I had to wait weeks, even months, when I got to a new school.

On this day the feeling of acceptance was the best. I think Jesus was there for sure. Jesus said, 'Let the little children come to me, and do not hinder them, for the kingdom of heaven belongs to such as these.' On this day, the angels had bestowed upon me the finest of gifts, sitting next to my peers with no division. We were all equal, and I chatted and got totally high on the sweeties. When I got home, I was possibly bouncing off the walls. Back to life as usual. My main problem was I was jumping out of my skin having possibly had too much raspberry lemonade and lollies and cakes.

The bridge

This one time, it was a warm summer's day and Des and Joe took us all for a drive out of town to a well-known watering hole. The watering hole was called Tom's Bridge. It was a popular picnic spot usually frequented by the locals, and a place where in the heat of summer, the locals cooled off in the river's icy water. Eventually, it was closed off due to a few drownings and near misses. The river ran under a bridge and there was lots of shade. Water was a must during the hot summers. My little sister and I couldn't wait to get into the water. We were so hot and had left Mum on the riverbank with her friends. I remember she was laughing and didn't seem so lonely. She was socialising with friends and drinking a few beers. I remember knowing she could see us, and we followed her instructions of staying in the shallow area.

We were playing in ankle-deep water, happy, just paddling and splashing around. It felt so nice, as it was a terribly hot summer's afternoon. I remember I was holding my sister's hand. I was an anxious child and always kept an eye out for her. I was also keeping an eye on Mum. When I'd last checked on her, she was chatting with her friends and one of them was sipping from a bottle of beer. Suddenly, my sister and I must've hit a sink hole or something, because down, down, down we went, and fast. My sister was trying to grab me for safety. She was clambering and climbing on me in a panic, trying to scramble to the surface. Survival is a built-in instinct. It drives you, and I know she just wanted to get her head above water, even if it meant climbing up me!

This was one of the most terrifying feelings of suffocation. I was drowning. I had no air left in my lungs and couldn't open my mouth. I had no idea how to swim, nor did my sister. Neither of us could've saved ourselves if we'd tried. We were both struggling, and I began to feel desperately tired. Minutes had passed, and in the end, I stopped resisting and gave into that sinking feeling. *Don't panic,* I thought, *we're going to drown.* Suddenly, from nowhere, the biggest pair of hands reached through the murky water and grabbed us, me with one hand, my sister with the other. A man placed us both in the ankle-deep water. What had felt like thirty minutes was in all likelihood two to three minutes. My sister coughed and started to cry. I looked to see mum still chatting and smiling, totally oblivious to what had just occurred. I looked to find the man who saved us. He was nowhere to be seen. I've always believed he was an angel sent to save us both.

We were drowning. It was like he'd come from nowhere, and then vanished. I think I dipped my toes in the water there one more time that afternoon before drying off in the sun. In all truth, it was really hard feeling on the outside of my family looking in. I never felt I was a part of the family. I never received affection from Mum and had to watch my little sister be the recipient of Mum's kisses and embraces. That was not only confusing as a child, but it also hurt me deeply. I felt so lost, and some days, I escaped by watching television and just keeping well and truly away from Mum. The older I became, the more I would take off. I loved the bushland. This was where I was my happiest. We lived in all rural areas so it wasn't hard to find a place where there was native scrub and creeks. Anything sensory was my thing. Touching, smelling, hearing, tasting. My senses were so strong that when I went to the bushland, I could smell the bull ants. I suppose this was a form of self-protection or disassociation. These escapades took me away from possibly being permanently damaged emotionally for the rest of my life. I have a curious, inquisitive mind. It was always wandering off. I was a complete dreamer.

Echidna in a suitcase

My precious sister had blue eyes and snow-white hair. It was clear Mum was blonde, as she was still putting dye in her hair. In comparison, I was skinny, lanky and dark-eyed with thin hair cut awfully short by my mother, often with a bowl on the top of my head. To top it off, I had an olive European complexion. I was always awkward and super fidgety, and my mother would tell me I had Saint Vitus' dance. More recently, I looked the word up on Google. It referred me to Sydenham's chorea, also known as chorea minor, which was historically referred to as St Vitus' dance. This condition is a disorder characterized by rapid, uncoordinated, jerking movements primarily affecting the face, hands and feet. I was a bag of nerves. I never slept well and Mum would often find me in hot, foamy lathers, crying in my sleep. I was a young child suffering from trauma, and additional layers were building up .

Living with Mum was more damaging than helpful. So not only did I look different and feel awkward, but I had some weird dance or hyperactivity that I couldn't control. After four years of being away from the orphanage and living from situation to situation with Mum, I finally mastered how to navigate my life around her moods. Her imagination was, at times, frightening and aggressive, and then there were other times when she would dress us both up and take us to the local picnic races to watch the horses. She'd talk about her parents' love for horses and how her father would lift her up at the races and point out the mighty Phar-Lap. The name Phar-Lap is comes from the Chinese or Thai word for lightning. Her father followed Tommy Woodcock and had some interaction with him as he was a trainer and, when he was a younger man, a jockey. She had also inherited her parents' love for horses, and she often talked about her own horse, Donny, her beautiful, white horse that would take them from Maribyrnong into the city of Melbourne on a jinker and cart. These were her memories before her life became abstract and distorted from the pain that followed her after the death of her brothers. Amongst other illnesses, she suffered from schizophrenia.

After a few years of getting to know Mum, I was able to gauge her bad days and, sometimes, her better days. Some days were what I'd call ginger beer days. Mum made the best ginger beer. Once a fortnight, Mum would go off to do some shopping. Not having a car left her with two options: either carry the shopping home, which she did often, or, depending on where she bought her groceries, a free delivery was possible on certain days. A small white truck would pull up the driveway and deliver your goods packaged in brown paper bags. It was very ecofriendly back in those days. As we lived in a rural area, there were lots of bushy areas to explore, and if you had enough food you could go hide and be lost for days. The smells of pine needles, lemon-scented gum, and eucalyptus trees was sometimes all I needed to stay sane. The bush was the best place for me to get lost in. These were my ginger beer days for sure; they were the times when I felt my happiest.

I think there is a rhythm or a pattern to most things in life. If Mum was going along okay, she'd be happy to take my little sister. That's when I knew all was okay. Mum would only be a few hours. On the days she didn't take my sister, she'd leave her at home with me and I never knew when Mum would be back. Having the responsibility of taking care of a child when you're just a kid yourself was sometimes hard work. My sister knew she could get away with things, and at times she could be a snitch and sook. She could get a little weepy and sulk without Mum. Either way, I took my responsibility very seriously, and I looked after her. As a big sister I loved and adored her. Many times, as I got older, I would go into battle for my little sister, and I was a big protector of her.

Looking back, I gathered Mum had hit rock bottom

by the time my little sister was born. She must've been Mum's salvation, so that's why I call her Salvation Jane, after a beautiful purple plant. Sally Jane was Mum's lifeline throughout the darkest times.

Mum was socially isolated from her community. Nana was a matriarch full of moral superiority, and who had been, for the most part, the guardian of three of the four older sisters. In those days, shame spoke louder than kindness. Jane was born three years after me, when Mum was forty-one. By this stage, Mum was getting older, and in those days too old to have another baby. Her health already wasn't great. Jane was her eighth child. I loved Jane regardless. Still, if anything went awry, she'd tell Mum and it would bite me on the backside, usually in the shape of a jug cord, tea pot, or whatever was in close proximity when Mum snapped and lost control. Mum was often not in control of her own mood swings, and yet when she told me stories of her many happy times, I was completely captivated. My mother had this look when she was just about to go off, and at these times I would slither away like a slug and hide.

There were many patterns I tried to navigate myself around; other times, I had no hope. If Mum's anxiety was building, and she left Jane with me, I knew she'd be gone a while, sometimes all day and not home till dark. Sometimes, there was no food in the house. Back in the 1970s there was no takeaway, other than fish and chips. The times when she was gone all day, I don't think Mum was thinking about us. I think she was just wanting to get as far away from me as possible and that's how the day went along. I just grew to accept it. I never understood, exactly, whether these days were free of stress or just stressful days, until the day was done. Only now, knowing more about mental health, do I realise that Mum was using alcohol to self-medicate and calm her nerves and to relieve her anxieties. But in actual fact, the outcome was quite the opposite with the alcohol possibly leaving her feeling more depressed and anxious and with less money than she left the house with.

It was on Mum's so-called 'shopping days' that I'd wander off. Not so far from where we lived, on the outskirts of town, about a kilometre away from the highway, I'd stumbled upon a curved dirt track that meandered into bush vegetation. The bush was in close proximity to the highway and houses and it was pretty much untouched. I'd get lost in there for hours upon hours. I loved tadpoling and doing what kids do, exploring or hanging. I loved the sounds of the bush, pobblebonk frogs and the sounds of their croaks, determining the type of frog. They were such soothing sounds, and I loved collecting frog eggs. Watching the little tadpoles wriggling. These activities intrigued my scientific senses as I'd watch the tadpoles transform before my eyes. I foraged for feathers from birds like hawks and wrens, and just scavenged for all sorts of other things. It was a pastime that gave me something to focus on, an escape. I could smell bull ants, and to this day, still can. They have a particular aroma, which smells like pine sol or lemon gumtree. My eyes were alert and sharp. Often, I would scope the trees' branches. If I saw a cocoon hanging, or a bird nest, I would leave them as they were, not moving or altering their natural state. I would also look to the ground to find anything of interest, such as fallen bird nests or blue green eggs or unusual stones or granite with a sparkle in it. Straight in the pocket they'd go. I loved the freedom, the smells, talking out loud, poking holes in trees, drawing in the dirt and yelling out 'Koo-wee!' I'd run around the bush, unafraid. This was my regular place to get lost in while Mum was having a 'shopping day.'

On one particular day, I was stuck with my little sister and we were heading there when I ran into my friend, Daisy. Daisy was my only friend at the time and I was so glad when I met her. She lived up the road from us and came from a large mob. She'd been kind and helpful when other members of her mob scared me and my sister as we'd walked home from the shops one time. They wanted our money, but I knew if I gave it to them I'd get a hiding from Mum, so I held onto it. Daisy courageously stepped in and told them to bugger off and leave us alone. They did so. Sometimes, I would see her and we'd play together.

One hot afternoon, I decided to take her home after I'd been to the swimming pool and ran into her. The look on Mum's face said it all. Daisy asked if she could go to our toilet and was gone a little while. When she returned, we had a drink together of homemade happy aide. After she left Mum went totally ballistic, frantically cleaning the toilet with her gloves on and disinfectant out.

'What's all the fuss Mum?' I asked.

'You're hanging out with Aboriginals!' she snapped, without hesitation.

Daisy was sweet and friendly, and she never showed me any bias. Still, from then on, I never brought her home again. I'd just wait until I ran into her. This particular day was one of those days. And, like us, she wouldn't be missed. A funny little trio, we followed the usual dirt track until we came to a clearing where things that had been dumped, like old tyres, bottles, clothes, etcetera. The plan was that we would eat our stale sandwiches, along with some of Mum's homemade ginger beer. She made good old-fashioned ginger beer. She had this way of doing it. She'd take an old jam jar and grind ginger and sugar into it. She'd then fill up some old beer bottles, usually about a dozen, and then she'd put these highly explosive gassy contents under the house. One by one, we'd pull them out over summer.

I would have to say the taste of this ginger beer was delicious. As I've gotten older I've tried to master her brewing, but no recipe has ever come close to the taste, and I haven't nailed it yet. One day I'll get it right. I also think maybe the sugar she used in the 1970s made the difference, or maybe it was just the taste of innocence and the times that will never come again, maybe like the ginger beer. Anyway, as we sat in the clearing, we poured out our goodies and shared them. Daisy liked the ginger beer, but my sister was dead scared of me pulling the cork from the bottle. She feared it was all shaken up from the walk, and began to fuss. After lunch, we had a lovely time eating juicy grass and just chatting, when my sister found this brown suitcase which had been dumped in the clearing.

'Come 'ere,' she motioned with her hands. 'Quick!'

I rolled my eyes at Daisy, but out of curiosity we walked over to see what Jane was glaring at. It was a suitcase.

'Open it,' Jane said. 'I'm not doing it. What if there's a dead body in it?'

'It's too small,' I replied.

Daisy, brave and gallant, stepped forward and tipped the lid with her foot. Inside was something I'd never seen before.

'A porcupine?'

'No it isn't,' said Daisy. 'It's an echidna.'

We stood around for a while, wondering how this cute, spikey animal had come to be in a suitcase.

'Maybe it was someone's pet?' I said.

'It could've just headed into the suitcase to hide,' said Jane, quietly.

This sounded like a reasonable idea. We just assumed it was asleep like a bear hibernating. When it was time to go home, Jane didn't want to go. In fact, she put on quite the tantrum, and refused to leave without the suitcase as the echidna would be alone, and if we took it home with us, we could feed it. We all just gathered it was sleeping and wasn't already dead. To bribe my sister to walk back home and not tell Mum about our little trip with my new friend Daisy, I carried the suitcase home. When we got home it was getting dark and Jane and I were hungry. Mum wasn't back yet, and Jane started to cry. I put on the television to calm her and went to make a sandwich. I began to worry about Mum's whereabouts and got on with getting ready for bed. Eventually, Mum returned home in a taxi, rolling in drunk.

By this stage, Jane and I had forgotten about the suitcase and the creature inside. We kept it that much of a secret, we forgot about it ourselves. We weren't meant to be away from the house. So it was never mentioned. Weeks later, Mum kept complaining of this terrible smell. We didn't know what she was talking about. She kept wandering about the house, sniffing, saying, 'Something's dead.' We were so young, we didn't understand, and we certainly didn't connect the dots until Mum found the suitcase and opened it. The echidna was well and truly dead by this stage. I recognised then that it must've been someone's dead pet dumped in the clearing. Who really knows? Salvation cried, and then I came up with a plan for a funeral. We had a funeral with hymns, a native floral tribute of flowers, and a cross of gumtree twigs put together with some old twine. Goodbye, echidna in a suitcase.

Part Three
TEENAGE YEARS

Brothers, boxing and ABBA

When we finally left the Moe area, we were given a ministry home in Morwell as Mum was finally eligible for the pension. By now, times had changed and in 1973 Social Services had introduced the Supporting Mother's Pension for women who were married without a supporting partner. It was very progressive for the times, and it took Queen Elizabeth to pass this new big change. This meant Mum was given support in all areas, including housing. The new area was familiar territory for me, as one of my older sisters used to live across the road from the house we moved into. We'd visited the street a few times when one of my nephews was a baby, and this familiarity made me feel more settled. Although not much had changed with the emotional bonds between Mum and I, my sister Jane and I had formed a closer bond, especially as I was the one who cared for her when Mum was physically or mentally unwell. Our home was on a slanted block, a typical weatherboarded home. The frontage of the house was at street level. The back was high up with a decent set of stairs, possibly eight stairs or more. I recall getting a Bambi mix of seeds for a gift in a birthday card. I planted them at the base of the stairs. All types of little seeds grew and reseeded for a few years after this. There was a great view from this back porch across to the old Melbourne Road and the old football ground. It was a great, wide vista of many things. Winter was very cold there and it was nothing to find washing stiff as a board on a cold frosty morning.

We had a little tin garden shed out back which we liked to play in. During the day, it was our cubby, and then late afternoon/evening in the warmer months. This became our stage. We both loved the band Abba and pretended to be an Abba cover band. I think this brought us even closer. I became Freda. I had dark eyes and hair and Jane was a perfect Agnetha with her dolly cut hairdo. Once our makeshift stage was set, we performed on the top of the shed in front of our corgi called Porky, and before him, Tinkerbelle.

As our live gigs became popular, other neighbourhood kids would turn up and watch and then perform along with us. We finally found our niche. I always loved music and singing was something I could do. 'Dancing Queen,' 'Fernando.' You name it, we sang it. As usual, I also got to know my surroundings. I easily found the pine forest, the billabong and the bushland areas. Again, finding my retreat, my respite, and a place to hide and get lost in for hours and hours. I made a few friends here, too, and sometimes we would get lost together. We'd lay on the ground and watch the clouds and talk about their formations as they morphed into different shapes and animals. I felt more settled than I had for years. I had my own room and eventually my brothers came home from the boys' home. They were the strangers this time. My older brother, Peter, was angry.

Often Mum and Pete would come to loggerheads over many things. Clearly, she was unwell. He was troubled for some time. The ongoing clashing between them was awkward to hear, and to watch. My mother truly cherished her sons; she just hoped for their love and approval. The tension would build up. It's sad to say this, but in the end it was better when Peter left. Things were getting so out of hand. He was clearly angry, and for good reason, after having spent twelve years in a Catholic institution. He had learnt well how to taunt me and my sister, often referring to me as Milo, due to my olive skin. Or, we were Rat Shit and Cat Shit. At times it didn't feel that nice to be tormented by him. No one knew how to talk about the time locked away in institutions. We all played a role in covering up this secret. A history in institutions was often confused with living in a prison. Only now does the general public understand that children were the vulnerable ones and subjected to awful conditions. Instead, we hid this, not wanting others to know our puzzling backgrounds. He would superimpose Mum's peculiar behaviours with a broad brush. This incited more tension. It must've been hard for them both.

It was hard enough for me trying to ignore Mum's irritating plucking. I hated it. She would pluck out a hair from her head, look at it and throw it to the ground. Ironically, she was a clean freak! She kept the house spotless. This was Mum's undoing, as it was the very reason she bought the vacuum cleaner in the first place, leading her into debt and us to the orphanage. I don't think Mum meant to be so unstable, and for a little while having the boys home seemed to put us on the map with the rest of the family. We were suddenly visited by the older sisters. I enjoyed having my brothers around. It took the pressure off Jane and me, for a while, and my teenage eyes were opened to new things, like boxing. Both my brothers previously boxed. If I'd been a boy I might've taken up the sport.

Peter, my oldest brother, was photographed with the great Lionel Rose at Festival Hall in the late 1960s. I still have the write up in the paper about Mr Rose being given an electric shaver, which at the time was an expensive gift. Peter was picked out of the orphanage boys to present this shaver, even though two of his front teeth were missing. He was a good little boxer and it would've been a privilege for him to give this gift to Lionel, who was his idol and a legend with fifty-three fights and forty-two wins.

Lionel Rose was a bantam weight boxer and someone all Australians were proud of. He was in the final selection for the 1964 Tokyo Olympics, but missed out by an inch. A teenager when he started his boxing career, Lionel was ten years, or more, older than my brother when the photo was taken. Both my brothers idolised him. They'd seen him at Festival Hall on a few occasions where they, themselves, learnt to box like many boys in the boys' home.

When Peter left the boys' home in the 1970s, his boxing came in handy as he belted a Christian Brother senseless. Clearly, Peter was like me, both of us being Taureans, the sign of the bull. We wait, we never forget, and when the time's right, we pounce. I'm guessing, too, that when he boxed the Christian Brother, he was making a statement. *Touch my younger brother, and I will be back*. This incident was never reported to the police and charges were never laid. I knew my brother to be strong in his youth, long before the heartache and loss broke his spirit. My brothers had their independence, were making money, and finally found freedom from the boys' home. They just blended into the community. No one knew their past. Like me, we just hid it.

After a few big altercations between Mum and Peter, both boys eventually moved out. They got a flat close to the main town. Not long after that, Peter pretty much got married. He was an attractive guy, so all my girlfriends thought, and it wasn't long before I had a new nephew. I adored his little boy, Jason, and so did my brother. This is when Peter changed. His anger seemed to dissolve, and he became a loving and beautiful father to his son. He loved being a dad and this role seemed to bring him peace, for a while. He adored his child, and it wasn't long before they were expecting a second child. It was a time of the big State Electrical Commission. Norm Gallagher helped to build up a powerful, national trade union organisation, the Builders and Labourers Federation (BLF). He was a General of both National Secretary from 1961-1990s. The working class, the labourers of the building industry and the subjugated, supported him well back then.

Peter really loved his wife's family and being with her perhaps calmed him. At the time, it seemed to me that both of my brothers were free from Mum's illness and that for Jane and me, there was no reprieve. We were stuck. And this was true. Maybe my brothers were also stuck in a different sense, an emotional one.

After my brothers moved away, my other brother, Paul, who'd always been the compassionate, caring one, decided he didn't want anything to do with her. And then, in 1995, when

Peter suicided, Paul was already away from most of the family. He didn't want anything to do with me, or a few others, at all.

He never came to Mum's funeral. I heard he held her accountable for all of his and Peter's losses. It's funny how Peter came out of the boy's home angry, and yet became so kind and caring, and my other brother, Paul, who was always kind, became hard-hearted. It's sad the impact the state had on my brothers. To this day, I will never fully know or understand the pain and trauma they suffered at the hands of institutionalised life. No child should ever be made victim to the needs of superiority. And, although I do know how very hard Mum tried to protect us, she was already victim to a heartless system where she had no voice or influence.

The fact remains the same. Mum was getting us back. Once the government social services were involved, we became in control of our fate. The older, more senior members of my family corresponded with social services. Mum had no credibility compared to the police, the social workers, the nuns, the church. These roles are held by everyday people who, for some reason or another, succumbed to their own power and desires, following rules and regulations that took advantage of others for reasons unbeknown to even them. For those in positions of moral respect, they couldn't even follow their own value system and stick to simple biblical concepts of stoicism and self-control. They had to touch what wasn't theirs to have. They had to interfere with the minds, hearts and bodies of the most vulnerable in their care. The frustration lies in the now uncovered facts that those who were uplifted and 'supposedly' trustworthy became the very epitome of dishonesty and corruption. Through the revealing of the sexual abuse scandals throughout the Catholic Church and other places of religion or power, the decent, ethical people have fallen out of the common man's approval. They are further from God and closer to Satan. Corruption and cover ups are now well documented in these modern times.

The suffering of myself, my brothers, and countless others, is ongoing, particularly where perpetrators have remained unaccountable for the psychological and emotional damage caused to individuals, families, and societies that have been affected by their abuse to this day.

The whole brushing over of men's behaviour compared to women's is abhorrent and lives on even in our modern times. Even today in the twenty-first century, fathers cannot be forced to be accountable for their children, no matter how many in the brood, with some men continuing to act irresponsibly for their actions while sullying the name of women. Imagine then, how difficult this was in the 1950s and 1960s where, if women even looked at men flirtatiously, they were considered whores, not to mention individuals being whisked away from their upper-class family and taken to some 'house' in the country to have their baby out of wedlock.

In Mum's case, she wasn't even out of wedlock when she had her first four children. It was only after the girls' father, struggling with what we know now as post-traumatic stress disorder from being a war veteran, went AWOL. The war was not Mum's fault, yet throughout her history Mum's name was ruined as if she were responsible for all of society's problems, many of which she seemed to be bear the brunt. The facts are, my mother fell through the cracks only to be swept up and used from all sides, including the State services. She was in the perfect position for receiving compassionate, Christian help, but instead was the recipient of cold-hearted scorn and was continually dealt an unfair hand. Women will always burden the blame. It's the archetype of the mother to always wear the pain of the child, or in this case, a fickle and religious society. I go back to the statue in Rome that day in Saint Peter's and the way the Mother Mary looked at her son. The pain for mothers goes on. For men, it seems, the pain is quickly redirected and they move on without truly looking back.

Both of my brothers were good men, but they fell into the unpredictable hands of the Christian brothers, a religious order that was supposed to uphold Christian morals and behave with decency, respect and consideration to the boys in their care. This just wasn't the case. I too had many disappointments within my orphanage upbringing and with Mum. It's taken some time and many hours of processing; however, I've found the compassion to forgive Mum. I looked at the reasons why she acted the way she did. I tried to understand her trauma. I considered those times in my own life when I acted without thinking, worn out, with no support, a solo mum myself, and with two kids of my own. Also, I'm finding, as I get older, that it's easier to identify how stress and tough times made Mum's illness rise up and attack. No one is free of making mistakes, and I think it's important to try and fix yourself and stop blaming others. I find this worked best for me.

As a young girl, Mum lived a sheltered life with a controlling mother. She was naïve, too trusting, and made many mistakes. I, myself, have made similar mistakes. We all have. In her honour, I'd say Mum did an incredible job under the circumstances.

Moving forward, I've come to believe the past shouldn't have such power in the now. For that to happen, forgiveness is the key.

No more eyebrows

From the very start of me returning from the orphanage and entering back into civilian life, I observed my four older sisters participate in a strange phenomenon. They always had a pair of tweezers at hand ready to pluck at either facial hair or other hair. Mum was also a plucker, due to her condition, trichotillomania, a hair-pulling disorder. Often mental illness comes with secondary, and third, and fourth issues. Mum couldn't stop pulling at her hair and it drove most of us crazy. I can't even describe how unnerving these repetitive movements were. I would escape by watching television, but even then I could still see her through the corner of my eye, plucking and pulling at her tiny hairs. After years of this illness, Mum became bald. Convinced there could be some hairy issues to face later in life, I was fearful about my own hairiness. Thankfully, the hair never sprouted in the same way for me as it did for my older sisters. It's not like they all sat plucking together as if they were making a quilt. It just seemed that when I was with them, usually individually, they always had a pair of tweezers in hand.

As I've always stood back to observe people, I didn't find it peculiar that I noticed this. I think it's simply one of my idiosyncratic perceptions of behaviours. To me, there was always a hierarchy of the hen house. These sisters were like hens, and there was an obvious pecking order. I found it amusing how they'd cluck away, pluck at their hairs, and hen-peck one another. As I entered my teenage years, I was truly relieved to realise I was unique. I was different from them due to my inability to grow dander. I was happy to not have it on my lip or face, better still, there was no painful clicking of tweezers. It was a dream come true. We all had the same mother, but thankfully, not the same genetic dispositions or idiosyncrasies. I'm in my fifties now and there is still no big dander of facial hair. This is such a relief, because, seriously, I do not like feeling pain. Plucking at hairs is often a painful exercise, regardless of my Italian bloodline. I had no extra fur or fluff on my face or chest. Differences have their advantages. I may not have been fair in colour, but to this day I have never been a plucker.

My sisters were all attractive, and as a girl and teenager, I was totally eclipsed by their beauty. I looked up to each and every one of them. They were all really gorgeous-looking women.

They inherited this from Mum and their own father had been tall and handsome. I hoped to be just a little like one of them, which is probably why I let my sister Mary give me an extreme makeover when I was twelve years old. Her extreme makeover turned out to be a flop. I was truly plucked.

My eyebrows were plucked, while her knee rested on my chest. This gave her extra leverage. She tried to dye my hair blonde; it turned a carroty blonde colour. When I arrived home, Mum was not impressed. Neither was I. After the hair started to grow out, I looked like a multi-coloured ferret, or Cruella de Vil. I looked awful. Another time, and after watching my sister shave her face, I later mimicked her by using my brother's razor, which I found in the bathroom. Oh boy. I accidentally shaved half an eyebrow off. This looked so silly, so I thought I'd solve the problem by disposing of the other eyebrow.

I was in a hurry to get to my friend's house, as sometimes her mum gave us a lift, so to mask my bald eyebrows, I used my mother's black eyebrow pencil and drew them in. I looked like a strange version of the silent French mime artist and performer, Marcel Marceau. I loved watching him as a kid pulling on pretend rope, his hands out like he was climbing a big pane of glass. I have to chuckle as I write this as my buddies Mary and Sue broke out in laughter when they saw me. So did Sue's mother. 'What have you done!' she cried, with a caring kind of laughter.

Sue and I would spend hours while her mum meandered around without a care in the world. This woman was never in a real rush. 'No, not shopping with your mum!' I'd joke with Sue and Mary. Of course, I would tag along anyhow, as we could hang out downtown, regardless. What a sweetheart and kind person she was. She was an amazing mother, devoted to her four children. I had jet black eyebrows, which were all pencilled in the wrong position. Maybe too high, and definitely crooked to boot. Sue's mum tried to tidy me up. Her makeup was always perfect, and I trusted her expertise. She used a brown pencil instead of harsh black. She dropped us off to school in her big, green valiant Charger. There was no getting away with a blunder like this one. You just have to hope they grow back and quick. They did.

My friends had a little bit of fun with me. They were never nasty or kept tormenting me. I didn't feel I had to conceal or hide too much from them at all. The more vulnerable I felt around them, the more trust was built. We all had each other's backs as teenagers do. There was a natural comradeship. Besides, we talked more to each other than to anyone else. We lived so close that everyone knew the happenings, even with our doors shut. We all knew a little of what was behind them. We were a close-knit community, which I enjoyed. I became part of this community more than my mother, as I was the goffer girl. Whatever was needed, I ironed out the crinkles, well, as much as a young girl could. I fronted up to pay the accounts at the local shops, to the butchers, grocers. I was the negotiator.

My relationship with my sisters was at times really good. Then things would change in a heartbeat. As I got older, I started to become myself fully. There was definitely a pecking order. I believe this exists in all families, especially larger families where there are so many more dynamics to consider. This story has all been from my narrative. All I can say to protect all of my family is that, in large families that have experienced different traumas, these traumas trigger each individual differently. As I got older, possibly I took more after my paternal side unknowingly. I became more confident and was no longer that little vulnerable girl anymore. After my brother's suicide, triggers were going off frequently. It set many wheels in motion. I never really felt like I fitted in after this terrible event, and a shift in the chain links of a family, often makes big changes. After his death there was so many shifts in our family dynamics. I thought I had experienced it all, but this took pain to a different level.

Triggers are the unhealthiest displays of distress. I have dealt with this professionally via Schema therapy, to acknowledge the incident and what certain incidents triggered in me have taught me that I am only accountable for my own actions. Mentally, I could not be there anymore or keep subjecting myself to any more patterns of abuse or unhealthy events.

My sister who was in the children's home with me was nine years my senior. Most of the time she displayed mixed emotions towards me, ranging from anger, disapproval, to pleasantness. These days I understand much more, and I have compassion for her own suffering and her traumas. I have compassion for all the other children who came before and after me because I understand the impact that these institutions have on so many lives. After many years of blaming myself for somehow upsetting my sister, distance became the healthiest way to cope. We all play our part in the drama. It is all very histrionic. In the end I removed myself cold turkey, and guess what? The drama was gone.

Back in that past lifetime, my main saving grace was, for most of the time, my malleable bubble. If I was away from danger and not scanning life for external safety cues, I was definitely a dreamer. I walked about in some transcendental way. My mind would just float around somewhere. There was a difference to our imprisonment. She was taken at nine I was taken at six months old. I knew nothing much but this harsh environment. My other poor siblings were introduced to pain that they had never ever experienced before. I just grew up in it. It is no wonder that my beautiful brother's life became unstable as a result of a very dysfunctional relationship. He was always concerned about his children and his long fight to always be a caring and loving father. His partner's divisive ways of trying to separate him from his children from a previous relationship had worn him down. She ring-barked him, like a tree. After a while the tree will die, and he did. We will never forget him, a life that was ring-barked by thirty-nine years of age and a majority of this time spent in institutional care. There was nothing rough or unkind about my brother. He was handsome and kind and witty.

I tried to help him by opening my doors to him and his little kids that he so longed to see, but he was falling into an abyss of heavy depression. It was obvious he felt disempowered. The previous time with the so-called Christian Brothers at the boys' home and those very oppressed feelings took him in the end. Helplessly, I watched his failing mental health. He was drawn back to her. She had the best pawns: two beautiful little toddlers. He had known her three months before the first was announced and then, she had the next baby within a year after. Mistakes rarely happen like this to a woman of thirty-eight years of age. She already had two teenage boys. I think it takes two to tango. What I struggled with was her using her two little ones over his previous children. After he died this very same women had two other partners, and guess what? You guessed it. The black widow. A toxic dark energy around men.

After reading Nana's letters in my wardship files to the Catholic nuns about the birth of my youngest sister Jane, I can understand the confusion she must have felt about many things back then, including me. One letter requested for the nuns to ensure that Mum would not be allowed to see us, as it would affect my older sister Mary as she is a very moral child. My poor mum was not immoral, she was vulnerable and struggling with another newborn, Salvation Jane. The Church, my older sisters, and the matriarch said it was immoral. Making everyone's life more difficult and no chance of reunification under those circumstances.

I only became aware of my older sisters after I left the children's home. There had been no memories of them ever as a small child. I do not think they all visited much. I would have remembered this. It was more my observations about them throughout life and getting to know them that hardened and protected me from getting too close.

I think the damage was done possibly before I was born. Many different genetics play a role in many different personality traits. Now that I know my biological father, I can see for the very first time in my life how I relate to his strong determined nature. Genetics play a very big role in our health and who we are, along with our experiences in life. Personalities have nothing to do with star signs, this I am very sure of.

There were some short-lived times of care shown by each of them. Usually, this occurred during a shift of power between them within the hierarchy of the hen house. Consistent kindness or caring towards me or each other was never maintained for long. Somehow, the relationships always ended harshly. As I became older and more independent, I started to notice this more and more. As a child I watched them interact with each other and it was not always pleasant. I could always sense their need for power, judgment, and control. Especially if you didn't toe the moral line, were different, or simply wanted to have your own freedom or sense of independence. My experience with them was akin to the feeling of a rug being pulled out from under a person.

A manufacturer's dream

When we returned home after Mum's hysterectomy, things seemed to go from bad to worse. I realise now that everything was different living with a parent with mental illness; a child is not allowed to be a child. I was forced to step up, and often. I complied with the role. I was the one who paid my mother's debts, the front man, the one who saw their smiles when paid or wore the disappointment if funds were running low. I learnt about money and how to navigate my way around paying the bills. Mum ran a line of credit with the butcher and with Spiros from the little local supermarket. She did this to make ends meet. Even though we were poor, I believe we could still carry ourselves with a certain amount of self-respect. I learnt this from Mum, who, although mentally ill, still had dignity. She never liked to owe anyone anything, no matter what. Even though I may have visited the shopkeepers to make the payments, it was Mum's minimal funds that paid the debt to the shops. Still, I didn't like the butcher. He came from an Italian background. He was very tall and imposing, he could be very serious like Don Corleone from *The Godfather* and would wash his bloody hands while I watched the blood drip into his stark white sink. I addressed him as Mr Frank. He was happy when the money was returned and the line of credit was paid off. Other times, if I had to face him without the money, he would often talk in broken English and gesture with his hands as he jerked his head. 'When she 'ave da money?' he'd quiz me.

'Next pension.' Then as quickly as I arrived, I would shoot out the door.

In the 1970s, progress was abundant across the landscape. Latrobe Valley, where I lived as a teenager, was a manufacturer's dream, and the infrastructure was a well-planned, thought-out process. There were plenty of factories within the Latrobe Valley region: the Australian Paper Mill, the Brickworks and Cement Factory, and the rag trade was big, to boot. Traralgon, where I was born, was put firmly on the map with the progressive Loy Yang Power Station being built between the 1970s and 1980s. The name Traralgon comes directly from the Aboriginal Gunnai language. Tarra means 'river' and Algon means 'little fish.'

The place grew fast, and by 1964, it was already progressive enough to be called a city. Morwell was to wait another thirty years to be recognised with the same status. The macroeconomics of the region were in full swing from around the 1970s onwards. Everyone had a job. There was mass producing of brown coal, paper, cement, clothing and shoes. Families were building into their dreams. There was nothing that wasn't built or being made in this area, or better still, in Australia. There were no issues around systemic unemployment for three or more decades beyond the 1970s. Unemployment rates were low. Hardly anyone was on the dole. Everybody worked hard, especially the new migrants, who worked even harder than the true-blue Aussies of the day. Many women worked in factories with their heads down and bums up, never talking much to anyone at all. The opportunity to build a new and better life in the thriving metropolis of the Latrobe Valley was very real. Many new migrants found this area appealing as it showed promise, especially after the war. A chance to get that bit of land. To move forward, build a life. They were also very hard times for many single mums, as they were a minority. There was no help, other than a hand out from Saint Vincent DePaul's, and judgements were made if you could not make ends meet.

Ironically, Mum, Jane and I lived hand to mouth on offal and very common cuts of meat, such as pressed ox tongue, tripe, sausages. Nothing flashy, unlike my friends who had a nice roast on a Sunday.

My friend, Brenda, who I met at sixteen, had a Sunday roast with her mother and father. A normal family. We met via my first boyfriend as she lived down the road from his home, possibly six doors down. Her father was Stan Mounsey. He was well respected. A war hero. He had been a Prisoner of War (POW) in Shanghai for years. I had the upmost respect for him. He also taught me how to stop my terrible blood noses. After all, he knew his craft. Tough hardly describes a man of his brave calibre. There was a shed erected by the Morwell RSL in his honour because he trained many of the local boys in boxing. Stan was great friends with Frank Oakes and had met his son-in-law Lionel Rose. In the early days, many migrant families often had a very hard time of it once they had arrived in Australia. One migrant's Italian mother showed up to Stan with her son. He was being bullied at school. His mother requested Stan assist her boy with a few boxing techniques. The rest of it was history. Rocky Mattioli became the former Middleweight Boxing World Champion. He took to Stan's craft of boxing very organically. Stan started training Rocky Mattioli at the age of sixteen. The boy was a natural, and I'm guessing no one ever picked on him again. He had over seventy-five fights and won sixty-five welterweight titles. Not bad for a teenage boy from Morwell.

My father, a Calabrian man, also came out in the 1950s. DNA was leading to a family I did not know. I was now finding out more and more. His family settled in the Latrobe Valley. Finally, I had made contact with a possible second or first cousin, and his wife. As soon as I arrived at the fruit shop, my perspective changed. There on the wall was a photograph of the man's father. That's when I knew, instinctively: this man is not my cousin, but my half-brother. Granted, we hadn't embarked on the DNA test yet, but I just knew. Looking at the photo was like looking at a mirror. All I could see was myself in the face. All of my life, I'd searched for my father and potentially here he was in black and white, a masculine version of myself. He had attractive brown eyes, and a small mouth. Everything about him was me.

I spoke to the supposed cousin. 'I think you're my brother, not my cousin.' He was surprised but remained jovial and agreed to my wish to organise a DNA test. Like the other test, I sent it to Vancouver, Canada. It came back a strong match of 99.6%. Half-siblings. Imagine it! Here I was in my fifties with many years of never knowing who my father was and being faced with the reality that I had found him. I was so happy and excited. My half-brother was not as convinced. He needed something more concrete. The poor guy was struggling with the revelation, and so asked for a second DNA test. This time, he wanted it to be conducted on Australian soil as he thought the data may have been tampered with in the lab in Vancouver, Canada. Of course, he's entitled to his opinion, and I understood his caution; however, I knew the test would come back the same. I also discovered he had a brother and that my father was still alive.

In all of my searching and hoping, I never imagined my father would still be alive, but he was. I never imagined this outcome. It is more than I hoped for. They say the truth always rises to the surface, and in this case, I'm absolutely certain it will. The big question, which I've continually found myself asking over my life may soon be answered. I'm trying to be patient with the answer, but it's not easy. Nothing about my life had been easy.

Escaping thunder road

I remember it was nearly the school holidays this one Saturday morning when Mum was in a terrible mood. She started ranting about the bikes we'd been given for Christmas the year I made my First Communion. Her grandmother in England had died, and Mum received some money. She purchased a blue bike for Jane, and mine was emerald green, like my birth stone for May. I loved my bike. It was liberating. I loved riding my bike too, although I'd mislaid my puncture kit as I remembered it had a flat tyre on this particular day.

'I got you bikes, and they're rusting in the shed. You never ride them!'

Next, Mum began the name calling again. This had been happening on and off. To this day I don't know why she started rambling about the bikes, but something had clearly set her off. Maybe one of the messages, which she said came over the radio? She always had a transistor radio glued to her ear all night. Surely, she must've struggled with these ongoing messages and banter that she received via the radio. It was so abstract. She was hardly sleeping at all, up all night talking to herself. As an eleven-year-old girl, I had no understanding of mental illness. Possibly, the isolation was a cause, but to this day, I don't know what set her on this rampage. I just thought she loathed me a little more than usual; looking back, I wonder if it was her schizophrenia that sent her into a frenzy. She may've been hearing voices telling her to act out, or perhaps she was sleep deprived. Does it even matter now? I was always in the line of fire, and I knew this was one of those times that I couldn't escape. Once she started, it went on and on.

'You black bitch, with your beady black eyes. Beady-eyed bitch.'

I started to run. I knew if I headed under the house I might be safe until she calmed down. Just as I ran to open the little gate to crawl in under the house, Mum tackled me to the ground and pulled my hair. She started to hit at me and whip me with a belt and I was copping the buckles and it hurt. Jane stood there watching and crying as Mum belted me. I took the hits for us both; I always had. It was always my fault. I scrambled under the house, cowering like a scared dog and sobbed. We had one operational bike at the time, so I grabbed it from the little garden shed and went to do a runner, but Jane yelled, 'Do not leave me here!' My protective older sister kicked in and I got us both on the bike.

'We need to run away,' Jane exclaimed, roaring with sobs.

I agreed, and pedalled as fast as I could. I decided to ride ten or more miles to the next town to get help from one of my older sisters. We at least had one bike and I told my little sister if we saw a car, we'd hide in the bushes until it passed, and then we'd hop back on the bike. We went all the way on the old Melbourne Road to the next town. On the way there, I began to feel exhausted, and we were desperately thirsty. I'd pedalled for what seemed like hours. There were not many houses, mainly farms in the area at the time. But, finally, we got to a house where I could hear children playing.

I said to my little sister, 'Stay there in the bushes and I will ask for water.'

The house looked as if it were being built. A man with a thick Dutch accent came out of the shadows. When he saw me, he looked surprised to see a youngster all the way out there, in a development area, alone. I asked him for water, of which he gave me a recycled Tarax bottle. I thanked him politely and left. Years later, when I met my husband to be, he took me to his family home. It was the very home where the Dutch man, his father, had given me the water. It took years for me to tell my father-in-law this story. He remembered it clearly.

Jane and I glugged away at the water until it was gone.

I knew the road well and had figured out we were at least another hour away from my sister's home. She lived in Traralgon and we had come from Morwell. We'd ridden ten kilometres and there were three left to go. I knew they'd be the hardest, especially with my little sister on a bike that was too small for me. Determination kept me on track. I was on a mission to get us to a safe place. Clearly, we left Thunder Road in a hurry, frightened and scared. I call it Thunder Road because I was like a cowering, whipped dog looking for safety. The day was hot and the ride was a lot for an eleven-year-old to tackle, especially as I hadn't ridden for ages. I tried my best, but after a while, I was totally beyond riding any longer. I advised Jane to hop off and that we'd have to walk the rest of the way. We were just on the outskirts of town when I saw a car coming. Whilst ducking into the closest bush, I recognised the car. It was my brother-in-law's. We remained by the roadside and waved, frantically. The driver did a one eighty and pulled over. He was a little shocked to see us and I remember being growled at.

'What are you doing all the way out here?'

He was a really friendly and approachable man, and could clearly see my distress. He then saw my arms, and I lifted up my shirt.

'It hurts,' I said. 'I cannot see it, but it's sore.'

Quickly, he bundled us both, and the blue bike, into his white station wagon.

'I'll take you to your sister,' he said.

He told me how he was now running late, that he was taking his son, my nephew, to see the movie, *Charlotte's Web*. I had seen it at school a few weeks prior. It left me in a pool of tears. I knew my sister wouldn't be happy with any of us if they missed the show, so he took us to my other sister as that's where I was heading in any case. She was kind, but had a husband that also had bad mood swings. It's possible he had a mood disorder. She'd met him at a young age and he was older than her. He wanted the best for her, I'm sure, but more often than not, he treated her like a possession. She would tiptoe around him, giving in to all of his demands. He had her on a terribly tight lead and she was pretty much a prisoner in her own home. She was an absolute glamour girl and always presented herself so well, though. A beautiful-looking woman.

I myself felt awkward. As good as a stray dog. Everything about myself, at this time, was apprehensive. My second eldest sister was everything I wished I could be, and I was totally out of the genetic league. She was so pretty, a full-on picture of loveliness. When we arrived at her home, I felt awful about holding up my brother in law's family. To this day I don't know if they made it to the movie. I never asked. Again, I learnt to just say nothing. Once inside my sister's home, she didn't chide me or tell me off, she just popped us in the bath. I was filthy. After all, we'd ridden for a good four hours, stopping on and off, hiding in the bushes on the way. We both needed a scrub. My sister looked at my welted back and got my brother-in-law in. Fortunately, he was very good this day. He had good days. He never was really mean to us kids. He told my sister to put something on it. I still remember him saying, 'She'll be black and blue when the bruising comes out.'

Once Jane and I were washed up, my older sister tried to comb my hair into a style. She was kind to me that day. She gave us fairy bread and we were playing outside with their kids when my brother-in-law came and took a couple of photographs.

The other brother-in-law, the one who'd picked us up, was often the friendlier of the two. Although, we hardly saw either of them. It always felt as if we were last on the list of people to visit. I still look back at those photos and see the sadness in my face on that day. We were taken back to Mum's late that night, once it was dark. When we got home, I copped another belting.

Mum is institutionalised

About two weeks after this, Jane and I came home from school and were locked out. Both hungry, we sat at the back door outside our house, like two loyal pets, not sure what was happening. We must've waited for some time, as it was becoming dark when we saw lights pull into the driveway. It was my brother-in-law who worked as a psychiatric nurse.

'Where's Mum?' I asked.

'She's in the hospital,' he replied. 'She needs to get well.'

I later learnt that my older sisters and their husbands had finally decided to step up and help us. They'd had a family meeting and worked everything out, including the logistics of where Jane and I were to go. I was farmed out to a sister who made it very clear I was pretty much in the way. Mum was placed at the Larundel Psychiatric Institution, which was part of a larger mental health complex known as Mont Park. I was never taken to visit her. She was gone for around two months. I still feel that to recover, or be treated for a severe mental health disorder, you need time. These days, and even after working over a decade in mental health, I call it treat and street. Meaning, you go in to receive the treatment or medication and then get sent out into the world, in which sometimes there is nowhere safe to recover.

In those days, the medication and treatments were so severe, even getting Mum's medication sorted wasn't easy. The same issues are prevalent today. Medications that work on one patient may not have a positive effect on another. No, I'm not from a clinical background and don't have the expertise to make a professional judgement; however, I feel we're all individuals with our own experiences and different levels of trauma. Symptoms are grouped together to create a diagnostic picture, and I understand that trauma can cause illness, yet I still do not understand how treatment for individuals is often prescribed as a blanket effect with a one pill fits all response. One pill does not, actually, fit all. There are many factors that need consideration.

Mum was in her situation because of undiagnosed trauma, which was never addressed. On top of this, she was layered with more trauma that then impacted her personality and started to destroy who she was. I say this because Mum seemed to become, or develop, this other persona. I had only known her firstly as a mother who had no connection to me, as her rights as a mother had been taken away from her. Then, once released from the orphanage, I saw her, mainly, as a mentally unwell person who was continually emotionally unavailable ninety-five per cent of the time. When she returned from Mont Park, she'd experienced additional trauma and the medical treatment had left her like a zombie upon her arrival home. She was vulnerable, frail, and underweight. She had tremors from the oral medication, which made her have involuntary movements of rocking backwards and forwards. It took a few weeks of an unsteady situation to make sense of it all. Mum was vomiting and not sleeping, but not ranting either. She was definitely making more sense and her trichotillomania had stopped completely. For a short time after she came home, she seemed like a different woman.

She was my mother, and I mean my real mother, or the mother I'd imagined her to be. She began addressing me in a manner that was caring and respectful, instead of looking at me with distaste and hatefulness. I'd often avoided her gazing at me prior to this, as she'd look at me with such disfavour, visualizing me as someone who'd caused her substantial pain. Sadly, I'd inadvertently caused her so much pain from my conception. My birth had isolated her from her family and the small rural community she'd lived in. Within such a small community, no father came forward, and yet someone knew they had been with her. My mother clearly decided not to pursue my father. Or, she did and he turned his back, walked away, and possibly blamed someone else. During this period of Mum's life, I'm ninety-nine per cent sure my father must've seen her walking around as she was left trying to deal with the situation and shunned by a community that had no empathy for her.

It is my belief that the men who took advantage of her committed the true crime. The man is always the hero, and back then, the woman was painted in a red dress and called a scarlet, a tramp. I'm not sure if much has changed even in today's society.

The blame for Mum's life, her mental health, her choices, her illegitimate children, lay with many and was not solely hers, although it fell heavily on her shoulders. All she needed was someone kind to love her. In Mum's case, there were no winners, none at all. When she was discharged and deemed well enough to return home, from the Asylum. Back then, there was no support, or a recovery model.

I became a different type of carer. I was eleven years old and just a child myself. Left to care for my sister, and our mother. Again, we were left abandoned and alone isolated from the community. I was ashamed to bring this to anyone else's attention. A nurse visited weekly. It took years to unpack some of these experiences.

All I could do was be a good helper. I'd make her a cup of tea, mow the lawns, do anything to help. I thought after she came out of the mental institution that she'd be 'fixed.' Instead, she was truly broken. After she returned, she looked like Meryl Streep out of *Sophie's Choice*, with such meekness in her mannerisms and vulnerability in her eyes. God, it was the saddest visual I've ever seen. I cried for her defeat, for our loss. After a few more weeks, I caught glimpses of who she actually was before life's brutal pain had been laid on her, layer after layer. Brothers dying, betrayal by mother and significant others, domestic violence by husband, and a community that had ostracised and failed her in every respect, including the men who'd abandoned and isolated her. She was alone!

Looking back on our lives, I realised that no one ever invited Mum to anything. Maybe we really were not part of the community norms. I'd learnt from a young age in the children's home to push myself out there, regardless. If you have no parent or an advocate, you have to do it on your own. You swim, or drown. I've always been a swimmer and survivor. So was Mum. She lived through tough times, and like any cycle, and we are not talking alcohol or drug addiction, we are talking mental health and prescribed drugs, she relapsed. She started to tip the medication that was making her mentally well, but also physically unwell, down the loo. The cycle started all over again. This time, none of the family came.

Thankfully, I had some friends and their parents who were looking out for me. My friend across the road and her mother already had two daughters working in the clothing and shoe industry and a majority of my friends worked in these factories. My good friend, Sue, who'd been by my side since the age of eleven, also worked at the shoe factory. Though it was my other friend's mother, Maggie, who'd offered a light in the dark. She told me she'd get me a job and, eventually, I'd be able to move out of Mum's. With all of our homes being placed so closely together in a small tenement, the neighbouring houses could often hear the abuse. I would still scramble under the house, run anywhere, usually just to hide. The neighbours had heard blow for blow the abuse, which was obviously intensifying. My education was seriously derailed, and I figured education was not going to help me much at this time in my life. Not at all. And, as much as I had the inquisitive mind and desire to learn, I struggled to stay focused, especially with little or no sleep at night due to my Mum's worsening mental health, her radio on all night, again, and her ranting and raving.

Sometimes she would burst into my room, drag me out of bed and beat me over something random. Knives were being pulled out in the middle of the night. This one time, Mum had me up against the wall by a strong grip, spittle coming from her mouth. 'You black bitch with your beady black eyes!' she shouted.

At times, I was absolutely petrified. I thought I was a goner. I just wanted out of the misery. There was no ending to the physical and mental anguish, and I was also trying to protect my little sister, as well. We were both in danger. One other time, Mum cornered me in the bathroom with a broomstick and was going to give me a physical lesson on the birds and the bees. She was so scary during these episodes, and on that occasion I thought she might really inflict the worst pain on me. She would often harass me about being around boys, but I was scared of any intimacy and far too young to even want to go there. On this day, she threatened to give me a taste of what sex was about. I blacked out or fainted completely. My mind just could not cope anymore. It was flooded with visuals of panic and I felt worried and confused as to what I had actually done to upset her so much.

Another time, Mum sent me down the shops to pick up something for her. When I got there, my friends were hanging around and I got somewhat distracted by chatting to a few of them. It was all very innocent, just a meeting place we all hung around at. I think it started when I used to wait for Sue, or her sister, to finish at the local fish 'n' chip shop. Then, within a few years, there must have been a good twenty of us hanging around there. It was all very harmless, and we were no trouble to anyone. I loved this comradeship and the feeling of finally belonging to a community of friends. They were all good kids, and we all looked out for each other.

This day, and because I was taking so long, Mum came

walking down to find me. She came right up to me in front of my friends and pulled her wig off.

'You did this to me!' she screamed.

My friends were gobsmacked.

I felt mortified. Kids starting to become teenagers truthfully just want to fit in with their peers. She then turned and headed back down the road towards home. Not one of my friends, boys or girls, were mean about it. I gathered that once I was out of ear shot, they must've chatted about it. Heading home awfully fast with the bread and milk in hand, I was ashamed. Embarrassed did not come close to the humiliation that followed after some of these awkward events. Many things were spiralling and I had been quite the inward sad girl. Expressing all this would have never happened at this junction in the journey. No way was I going back to the children's home, or worse still, Winlaton Training Centre for defiant, bad girls. No, my plan was simple: just, die. I worked as a mental health practitioner for over a decade up until not so long ago. One of the questions workers might need to ask if a client was in an acute stage of depression was: do you have suicidal ideations? Do you have a plan? I had both. I was thirteen years old. It was on a Saturday night as my friends were all hanging out. Their parents trusted them enough to drop them off at the local cinema. Occasionally, we just stayed at a friend's house, playing records, chatting, just being kids and doing stuff. Again for some unreasonable weird excuse, I was not to hang out with my friend Sue and Mary and others. In my youthful head, entering the bridge of puberty, I couldn't cope anymore. This night I was quite resolute. I felt calm and peaceful about my decision. I wrote myself a wonderful script in my head. I put so much thought into finally being free from my life of absolute misery. Although, there were some minuscule threads of hope, they didn't feel momentous enough to force me to hold the life as I'd known. Other than my little sister, and my friends, I was okay and resolute to bid them all farewell.

I was at an age where my sheer existence relied on every word from within my friendship circle. My mask was definitely affixed when with my friends. I did not want them to truly see all this strange stuff I was dealing with.

After all, friends are the wind in your sails, and at thirteen, it's like every moment counts. Every word is so true, so important. I hid as much as I could from my friends. The boys we knew were often mean and immature. Like all young boys, they loved to stir us girls up given half the chance. We'd all hang at our local shop near my best friend's house. We were good friends and it was all very innocent. We talked about music, the latest vinyl albums, Skyhooks, Bowie and *Countdown*, the popular music show where we first heard the songs by Australian and international artists. Then, it was a rush to buy a vinyl single. Teenagers are just seamless and fit in, they don't want to be reminded of anything being different, or for that matter, weird. I had the single-parent family, and the very, very different.

Puberty makes you already feel weird enough with the endless plethora of issues that come hand in hand with adolescence, like the changes that take place such as the transforming parts of the body, periods, and acne. Now as I have matured and gotten much older, I realise the fragility of teenagers. They struggle, coming even from the securest of families. We continually hear on social media platforms about the death of many young people. In your fleeting time of youth, one or two bad experiences can leave a young person who hasn't had time to build any resilience at a total loss.

My friends were in many ways trusted to make many of those fundamental choices on their own, like using junior tampons. Nothing came easy for me. It was a continual embarrassment and any of these private discissions may as well have been a headline in the local Latrobe Valley Express. When I asked Mum if I could use them, she hit the roof. She flatly refused and said I was not a virgin; my brother's girlfriend, who was five years older than myself at the time, was very supportive. She sat with Mum and in a way, she could reach her in a caring, calm way. She explained the modern way of girls using tampons to my mum (we are talking late 1970s by now). My mum was born in 1924. Her mother was born in 1895. Then there is me, born in the 1962. The gaps for me were more like being a plane crossing the northern Atlantic Ocean, the Bermuda Triangle. If only I could be swallowed up and disappear.

Then came another problem for me when these cycles started. I became terrified of being in water during my period because Mum told me if I bathed or swam, I could die. This clearly had been passed down from my Victorian grandmothers' era. It was all weird and different. These peculiar ideologies went on for many years. Friends would wonder why I was totally off the radar at certain times in the summer months. The effects another person's beliefs systems can have in a very bizarre environment can have a lasting impression on an inexperienced girl. Usually, your first foundations are built on home life, then you go out into the world. Both of these initial experiences were abnormal in my mind. The children's home was the only environment I had known, mini militant life. There was nothing much normal in the institutional lifestyle. My mother's spiralling mental health left me with feeling as though I'd upset her and then feeling responsible for her explosive moods. Still, nothing was easy. Even the usual milestones for a young maturing girl came with obstinate conflicts. So, I sat on the edge of my bed holding a bottle of Mum's pills. I got up and said my goodbyes to Porky, our corgi, with distress. Then, I kissed Salvation's forehead and told her I loved her, and that things would be better now. She just said I'm tired and dozed back to sleep. I cried quietly in my room. Being a true romantic at heart, I felt like one of those glamorous actresses from one of the many movies I'd seen over the years. It's near funny when I think about it now, as if I was Cathy from *Wuthering Heights*, or Jean Turney from *The Ghost and Mrs Muir*. They died in such passionate, romantic manners. In no mistakable way was this a funny idealistic time. It was the very worst of times, crossing the bridge from childhood to puberty. I'd been deprived of love and affection and was navigating my youth without secure footholds or the necessary foundations of support, acceptance, and love that is on offer in most loving families. I knew what I was missing out on, because I'd seen this articulated in the families of my girlfriends. Even now, forty-three years later, the turmoil of my youth is difficult to talk about. My heart is heavy, as it was back then when I poured out half a bottle of Mum's pills and consumed them in one fell swoop.

Once swallowed, there was no turning back. The pills were in my stomach. Eventually, after sobbing myself to what I thought would be my death, I fell asleep. The next morning,

I awoke as thirsty as a sailor in a desert and definitely not dead, nor cold in my bed. I was alive. I think so many suicides end up different to mine, which turned out to be a complete dud, a placebo attempt. Even so, my teenage mind had turned a corner and made a very cognizant plan to survive. Young, malleable minds have such a passion to act without no understanding of consequences at all. Damn it. I was not going to give up on me! I would put my mind on emotional bail and stay focused and determined and move my sad, sorry arse forward. Education, or no education. By June, I would start work in the shoe factory. That had now become my only ticket out of the ongoing abuse. Anywhere but where I was, or had been, would suffice, and I was glad to be going where a few friends would be.

The shoe factory

I'd finished my first year of high school and one semester of my second year when a position came up at the shoe factory. I would start work and begin my road to independence. Mum was all for this because it meant money. The hardest thing was telling my Year 8 coordinator, Mr Andrew Blaire, the news. This remarkable teacher was instrumental to me and an essential role model during my times of self-doubt and confusion. At the time, Mr Blaire seemed to be the most inspirational teacher I'd ever had. He believed in me. This was a rare feeling. He never could've known the full impact or the depths of my misery or despair, even though I'd said a few things to him, things I didn't rightly understand myself that I was experiencing; it was often difficult to process or really get a handle on my situation. There's something to be said for the importance of a good, dedicated teacher. Although Mr Blaire never knew the extent of my personal situation and that leaving high school was the lifeline I needed, I owe my persistence in revisiting my education, as an adult, to him, and I will always be immensely grateful. Mr Blaire accepted my reasons for wanting to leave high school and gave me a send-off on leaving my year 8 class. It was a fantastic party, the second one in my life. As a leaving gift, I received a pair of rainbow toe socks, which were all the trend then, and Mr Blaire gave me a beautiful card with lovely words of kindness and beautiful artwork on the front of the card.

It was a copy of a painting called *Madonna and Child* by artist Jan Van Eyck. The painting is of the Madonna and a little baby boy. Madonna is depicted on her throne in a display of both realism and beauty. It is a visually powerful painting. The Madonna is seated elegantly, while her baby, who is clothed in a simple white scarf about his bottom half, sits upon her knee. The Madonna is educating the infant by showing him a book with pictures. She is cloaked in a ruby red robe, which indicates to me she is a woman in a position of power with knowledge to pass to her adoring infant son. Today, I still receive the very powerful message the card depicts. The baby boy in the picture would be about the same age as my grandson now, at the time of writing. This little memento of acknowledgment and care sits in a frame and has come everywhere with me since I was thirteen.

I started work at the shoe factory as a manual worker. One of my first jobs was actually stamping the code and size onto the shoe. It was like a stamping mechanism, and the most important part of the job was remembering to change the ribbon band after each batch of fifty shoes. We mainly made desert boots, boots, and decorative men's shoes suited to going to a wedding or somewhere fancy. I called them old gentlemen's shoes. Other than a priest, I never saw men in the area we lived wearing fancy footwear. Most of our orders for shoes went overseas, or to big fancy department stores. For a good few months, I stamped shoes. It was very repetitive and often outright mundane, and if I forgot to change the ribbon from white to red, or, to gold, depending on the shoe order, I had to sit down and scrape the old print off and start the entire boring process again.

As previously mentioned, I had one of my best friends there, Sue. I absolutely loved her, but boy did the manager dislike me. The only thing that kept me employed was my friends and a few good ladies at the factory who were also friends with the manager. I actually figured out one day that, as the youngest in the pecking order, the manager probably thought that if pushed hard enough the pressure would make me quit. But the opposite occurred. I was very strong-willed, and super determined, and I wasn't going to give in as easily as she'd hoped. After a while, and although I was in a position of gaining my independence, my earnings were nearly all going to Mum. She would grab my pay packet and leave me with ten per cent of what I earned. I did what she wanted until one day my brother told her that I'd worked hard and to leave me with something.

Meanwhile, Sue and my other friends and I were happy at the factory. Of course, she was a neat sewer and did everything requested of her. The boss sang her praises. Not me. She had me go into the tearoom before morning brew and lunch time. My task was to set out all the cups and make sure there was ample milk, sugar, tea, coffee, and biscuits. Then, after smoko, when the bell went, I was to wash up all the cups and put them away. She would give me a certain amount of time to do this, but I was literally on the clock and would be ripped into if I fell behind. When this happened, some of the other women would get upset with her as she didn't know when to stop. Little did she know, my new job was heaven compared to where I'd come from. I just kept robotically doing all my tasks, regardless. Betty the boss would up the ante by setting shittier tasks for me to do.

I had to clean the toilets, which I wasn't that happy about. I didn't want to swing a mop around the floor. Part of this job was also to clean the women's sanitary pads out of the Bunsen burner. In those days they weren't thrown in the sanitary bin. They went in a little gas burner, and you pushed a button or lit it with matches. It absolutely stank to high heavens and, honest to God, you could smell it from the bus depot next door. Some of the young workers would stir us up and say somebody's got their rags if they saw a plume of smoke pumping from the chimney. I was only fourteen at the time, and my rebellious side had started to emerge. After a while, I had a gut's full of the stinking, drunk boss lady. She was always sneaking out at lunch time in a cab to get a few pots or pints into her. A liquid lunch, it's called. Then, she'd come back to work, half tanked, and push certain ones around, including me.

After work, she'd meet up with her husband. They were a funny looking couple. He needed a bariatric stool, and she was the size of a twig, go figure. The two of them would drink the night away in the sportsman bar. I detested her, quite frankly. She would order me to make coffee and would always have her stinking Rothmans cigarettes, which came out of a red box, burning in an ash tray somewhere, often forgotten about, as she'd already have another one on the go. They stank like horse shit.

'Frances, get and make a coffee now, and make it hot!' she'd say.

This one time, with my friend Sue watching like some captive audience, I spat in Betty's coffee. Sue didn't laugh, but glared as if to say, 'Oh My God!' I handed the boss her coffee with a smile.

'Nice and hot,' I said.

'Nice and hot, mmm,' she replied.

I only did this terrible thing one time, but in my defence, she was discriminating me, treating me like a slave, and I hated my job cleaning the toilets. It was always freezing and my hands would turn purple from the cold. By this time, I'd started to act up. Some might say my switch was flicked, but I felt disempowered by this lady, and I was a young teenager. She was always sitting there with her smoke packet near Sue, accusing others of stealing her smokes. She knew my friend didn't smoke. Sue was honest, and I couldn't see how anyone would bother to steal her filthy cigarettes, anyway. After a while, I got fed up and grabbed the boss's Redhead matchsticks and stuck one in the tobacco end of a cigarette. Sue and I waited on tenterhooks for the big moment. We watched the boss slowly pull out a match and then sift through her packet, looking for which cigarette to take. It was like watching Russian roulette in an action movie, but this was with a cigarette. Which one was loaded? Was she safe for the time being?

Sure enough, kaboom! The cigarette took light, and it was quickly dispersed into the ashtray. Betty didn't have the vaguest idea of what just occurred. Silly old biddy. She was even oblivious to the tampering of her ciggies. Sue and I laughed when she walked off to nag some other poor victim, usually one of the Italian or Greek women. My friend was living life dangerously through me. During our breaks we would be in fits of laughter, safely having these little wicked secrets. Poor Sue copped it more as Betty hovered over her. Sue was always super nice, whereas I was glad I was on Betty's not-to-like list. She stank. I swear she never washed a day in her life. Hygiene was not high on the agenda, not at all. She had that awful nicotine stain between her fingers and dirty fingernails. She was a nose picker to boot. I didn't like alcohol, and she clearly was an alcoholic. She was about forty-two kilos, always wore stiletto shoes, and often had ladders running in her stockings. Sometimes those ladders might be at the front of her leg, as if she'd been on a bender the night before.

There was a distinctive chip in her front dentures and her lips were smacked with bright red lipstick. I visualised her getting into bed plastered and reaching to put her teeth in a jar of bleach, missing completely, them hitting the deck and breaking. Why spend money on a new set of teeth when beer was a better option to put in your mouth? Her hair was dark and short, which she wore in a cold wave perm, or, if she was being fancy, she'd have it set in curlers. Sometimes, she came to work in her curlers with a sheer net wrapped around them. What a sight! If only this woman could've seen herself giving everyone orders. She was a sight and smelt of booze, as she coughed all over any unlucky victim while giving them a lesson in sewing or a demonstration on beading or eyeleting a shoe. She was a constant fixture in the bar with her spouse.

I felt for the Italian and Greek women, as the boss would hinder them. I could hear them talking sometimes in their own language after she'd left them alone. As she continued to push me, I continued to push back, especially after all my demotions. I was gutsy, but not rude. Being bullied by this awful woman for three years was nothing. It was more annoying than awkward. She knew my mother from before I was born, and I reckon she had a bee in her bonnet about something.

After making me clean out the unburnt sanitary pads, Shirl, the union rep at the factory, called a big meeting during teatime. I knew the talk around the factory and saw how she treated the migrant women and anyone struggling. She wanted them to acknowledge her as the manager, the big boss. But, being in management does not earn you respect if you treat people under you with none. At the meeting Betty was told, in no uncertain terms, that if she didn't employ a tea lady and cleaner, we would all walk! Go on strike! The meeting was on the Thursday and that Friday night none of the ladies, who Betty usually caught up with from the factory for a beer, showed up after work. They went somewhere else to have their end of the week drink, and the boss was out in the cold getting a bit of her own medicine, for a change. By the following Monday, she was absolutely beside herself.

And then, a lovely lady retired and a new lady called Philippa started as the new tea lady. I was off the hook.

They say you reap what you sow, and Betty finally did get her just desserts. I would've been sixteen or so when I was with the ladies all sitting at the local boozer. We were in the lounge. Suddenly, there was a huge hype of activity.

'It's Betty. She's been killed!' said someone, running towards us.

Apparently, she'd taken a man's seat while he was at the bar. This way she could sit directly under the air conditioner, as it was a very hot summer's day. The story goes that the whole air conditioner unit fell out of the wall and landed smack on her head. The younger ones among us ran to the front of the hotel to have a gander where the ambulance was. She had a white bandage wrapped around her head and was stretched out on the stretcher waiting to be shipped off to hospital. She wasn't dead, but she was wailing in pain. Still, I held back my laughter, as I was never an unkind person. As the ambulance sped away with its sirens and lights ablaze, I fell quiet. I would never wish that on anyone. Fancy being that unlucky! When we all returned back to our lemonades, there was this uneasy quietness.

'I think you'll have to step up on Monday, Marg, and run the factory,' said Shirl.

Within seconds, we were in a fit of laugher. There wasn't a

dry eye in the lounge. Everyone, including the bartender, lost it. We all cried laughing. You had to be there, I guess. What a relief to laugh. I still laugh about this. On Monday, Betty was back at work, fag hanging from her mouth and a bandage wrapped around her head. I flew into the ladies' bathroom along with a few others and again we cried laughing.

Betty sued the hotel. Following this, another incident occurred as she was visiting the powder room. Her stiletto got caught in the seam of the carpet at the same hotel, and she fell and broke her arm. She went for compensation again. Alcohol had nothing to do with her issues. She was good at laying blame and not taking responsibility.

The doctor

For many years, I've struggled to speak about certain secrets that I've kept to myself, because I felt so conflicted and confused. I supressed my voice by attaching invisible chains and padlocks to lock those conflicts away. They are usually there to protect ourselves from any further distress. Or, we hold them so close to us we need a key to unlock them out of fear, or out of wanting to avoid judgement from others. Leaving home at a young age left me without the basic supports. Simple things like driving lessons, or homework help, or having support with you at the doctors. Just the things that a parent usually assists a teenager with until they're ready to be independent on their journey into the big wide world. Within my upbringing, I missed many steps. I had to be the one to step up and pull my socks up. To just do it. I had no one there to guide me as a young snip of a girl. Sure, I was street smart, and knew some things, but I definitely had to draw on any past experience to guide me towards becoming an adult. In many ways, I was completely unprepared.

One of my memories of needing to see the doctor was of one of my brothers. He often had issues with his shoulder, which would dislocate frequently. I would hear him yelling for help. On a few occasions, I helped to connect the shoulder back into place. This was done by quickly pulling and clicking the shoulder and stabilizing it. The pointy bone was visible and sticking out. I still have memories of how brave he seemed to be when faced with such pain. Slowly, I would push his shoulder blade toward the spine using my fingers sitting on it. I would wait, and as soon as I heard the clunk and saw my poor brother's relief, I knew the job was done. After many repeated instances of this painful condition, he finally followed through with a surgical procedure. I loved my brother. He had a lovely nature, and was always trying to be a good mentor, and I looked up to him.

Once I entered the work force, I quickly realised that if I was unwell and needed to take a sick day from work, I would need to produce a doctor's certificate to ensure I would be paid my sick leave entitlement. Naturally, I would do anything to avoid time off work; however, when I was so unwell, I just had to stay home. A certificate from the doctor was a necessity so that I wouldn't be financially disadvantaged any more than I already was. My wages back then were seventy-eight dollars and fifty cents a week. My rent or board fluctuated from twenty to forty dollars a week, and then there were food and bills. It was not easy meeting my weekly payments, but I managed. And more significantly, I've never been in debt.

Anyway, this one day on my walk home from the factory, I noticed a small medical clinic was now running and working there was the same surgeon that had treated my brother's dislocated shoulder. Although I had numerous recurring illnesses since childhood, such as hives, bloody noses, infected tonsils, and anaemia, I had little to no experience with doctors. If a doctor had been called to the children's home, a nun was present, or, once I returned to Mum's care, she would be there to get the diagnosis and collect the medicine. So, the positioning of this clinic came in handy, as I had easy access. It was within walking distance from home and work, and this ex-surgeon was a person I was familiar with.

I decided I would go to him if I needed to. This man had repaired my brother's shoulder and I instantly trusted him. Why wouldn't I? There was no need to worry. He had a wonderful reputation, and he'd even built my trust after a few consultations with him. I liked this GP. He was always friendly and welcoming. His large walnut wooden desk allowed distance between us as we sat and discussed what the ailment was and how best to treat it. We'd often sit for a while, and he was good at building rapport, being very harmonious and considerate, and although his office smelt musty, like stale aftershave soaked into the cloth furniture, he created a warm, friendly platform for a young teenage girl to feel comfortable in. There certainly was no need for concern or to feel wary in his presence, at the start. The first few medical conditions were dealt with efficiency and with a script written up and a certificate for work. Things were all above board for the first year. Then, I noticed a change with his medical approaches to my conditions. They started to take a strange turn, which left me baffled and scratching my head. I wondered if this was a normal consultation. Why did he have to see this, or do that? Still, I just thought it was best practice. He was the doctor. Doctors know best.

But then, things took an even stranger turn when I had a very sore ear and tonsillitis. At this consultation, I was directed to sit up so he could check my lung capacity, and then, I was asked to lay down on the bed. I didn't understand why, but I just followed his orders. Having been spoon-fed discipline from a young age, I was used to being obedient. Even so, my instincts were telling me to leave. Suddenly feeling trapped, I was unsure of how to say no. I couldn't be rude or say no to a doctor, could I? I'd trusted him with my health, with my life. Then, I felt him touch me in an area that had no relevance to tonsillitis. Like a petrified animal in a trance, I had an out-of-body experience. The predator had pounced, and I froze. I knew something was drastically wrong. My heart was pounding. I was so scared. I tried to say stop, but no words came from my mouth. Where had my vocal cords gone? Were they severed? Was I drugged? Say something! I couldn't. Nothing was coming out. Somehow, I snapped out of it, even though I was beyond fear. Like a jack rabbit, instinct kicked in, because next thing I know, I got up quickly, got my undergarments on, and without hesitation, I ran. I ran past the receptionist and out onto the street.

It was a blistering, freezing day: any colder and the tears I cried would've turned to icicles. As soon as I got home, I vomited. I felt dirty. I jumped straight in the shower. All I could smell was his stinking Old Spice like a smell deeply planted in my nose. I washed it all off. My underclothes, anything that was linked to him, was thrown away. Feeling frightened or threatened leaves you with three choices: fight, flee, or freeze. In this scenario, I experienced all three. I froze, I doubted my own mind. To flee was my second reaction. I fled. Then when his bill arrived, my fight kicked in. In the 1970s, a doctor was in a position of power equal in authority to a priest, or a policeman. But I never was paying his bill, never. He had sexually assaulted me. Like many young girls, I never told a soul. It must've been my fault, I thought. But then, a few years later at work, in the tearoom, not meaning to eavesdrop, I overheard a conversation. It turned out this doctor hadn't just assaulted me, there were others. He was never charged, to my knowledge. No young girl was going to step forward. I never did. It was something else to hide, one more layer. It just made me more silent and inward.

Moving

Mum agreed to my moving out when I met a lady who I thought was trustworthy. She worked at the shoe factory and at the time, it felt like she was offering me the lifeline I'd been hoping for. She mentioned to me one day how she'd spoken with her husband, and they were happy for me to move in with them as long as I paid board.

I'd made the big move, thinking I was going to get a nice room of my own, and I was excited about my first step towards independence and adulthood. What I did not account for was this couple's two-year-old daughter, who they stuck in my room way down the other end of the house. They actually had another two bedrooms, and when I hinted at needing to get a good night's sleep, the husband looked at me as if I was ungrateful. Every night, I gave the toddler her bottles and dummies. It was an absolute nightmare. During the day, I was the boss's slave, and then at night, I was the nanny, or live in au-pair. At the time, I just did what was asked of me. It was many years later, when I became a mother myself, that I realised how selfish that couple had been. They were in their late twenties, both of them getting a restful night of sleep, and here I was, awake, with a child that wasn't even mine. When I started to date my first boyfriend, I was given strict instructions to be home before midnight. I was late one time.

'One more time and you're out!' said the husband.

My boyfriend was older than me and we hung out for some time together. His mother adored me but his father's emotions toward me were very reserved. His family was from Scotland. His mother, Jessie, was the most pleasant lady, and his father was very much a product of his own harsh upbringing. He was born in the 1920s and everyone was a little unsure or scared of him. He was a man you didn't mess with. He demanded respect. Life hadn't been easy on new immigrants. They had moved to Australia from Scotland in the 1950s for a new job at the local State Electrical Commission. Regardless, the grown-up kids all showed him respect, even if they didn't agree with his point of view. He was an amputee and always sat in front of the house. Jessie was always in the kitchen or hanging out the window yelling 'Hello' or Come in' to the passing people going to the local milk bar or stream of shops just past their house. She was a dear lady, and the kettle was on 24/7. Her family adored her, as did I.

Being timid and polite, I would knock on the front door

and enter the house as opposed to coming and going through the back door. I think my boyfriend's father really liked me, as I remember one Saturday night just before the lotto draw, he said, 'You're okay for a mick,' meaning a Catholic.

Here I was in awe of my boyfriend. I had been around him at dances like ACDC or Skyhooks, but I was his younger brother's age. He had first kissed me at a dance when I was thirteen and even then, pretty much said he was going to wait for me. By this stage, I'd been away from Mum for a while, although living with the couple wasn't working out. When I meet up with my boyfriend again at sixteen, he came to get me and he was given a good talking to by the husband and her brother, you know, the usual. If you hurt her watch out, that kind of thing.

In the end, I got home late one night. It was all very innocent. He was very protective of me, as I'd gone with him to watch his brother who played in a local band. Afterwards, I had to wait for the roadie, my boyfriend, to pack up the equipment. I had to leave, all because I got home after midnight. Clearly, they were annoyed because they had to tend to their child's needs. They didn't care about me. I was about to be homeless all because this couple needed sleep and lacked accountability for their own child. I felt pretty awful about this as my friend from the shoe factory was a sweetheart, but her husband had some old-fashioned values, even though he took no issue with a sixteen-year-old looking after his daughter during the middle of the night or early in the mornings. After leaving the unpaid nanny job, I became a gypsy. I boarded and went from place to place until I found a flat at the back of someone's house. Then I moved towns to Sale, Myrtlebank. I was desperate for any security, so I even went back to the place I had run from. Discombobulated, I began to feel I was following in Mum's footsteps.

At this time, Mum was again very unwell. My little sister was now alone with her, and she was like me before I had reached puberty. She wasn't coping well. We were all a trainwreck. I had a chance to get a hairdressing apprenticeship, but Mum had to be certified to a mental health facility, which would make me the primary caregiver for my younger sister. I made many calls to my older sister begging for help. No one came. A seventeen-year-old looking after a fourteen-year-old. They were never coming to help, never. I left hairdressing for work in a pub kitchen as I needed enough money to look after us both. Eventually, I took my very unwell mother to a local country GP. and I had to certify my mum to Hobsons Park mental facility in Traralgon. It was horrendous. She screamed at me when I hitched a ride to see her after missing the train from Sale. Previously, she had been getting a depot antipsychotic injection after her stay at Mont Park. It contained a medicine called fluphenazine. This belongs to a group of medicines called 'phenothiazines' and they work by blocking the effect of a particular chemical in the brain. They are used as treatment for schizophrenia. A person who has this illness can often feel, see, or hear things which do not exist. These can include having strange and frightening thoughts, sometimes paranoid psychoses. Also, there may be changes in a person's behaviour or they might feel desperately alone. Sometimes a person with these symptoms may also feel tense, anxious or depressed. She also took Cogentin to counteract the awful side effects of the fluphenazine. This time around Mum was placed on a community treatment order and stayed on her medications, which settled her down. The ECT, electric shock treatment, was severe. Mum's memories were often misguided or misplaced even though her long-term memory was sharp. In her well times, I was able to collect more stories. Whenever I asked her about my beginnings, about how I came to be, she would be completely confused. A favourite memory I have of Mum during this time is when the younger of my brothers got married. She looked stunning on the day of the wedding. She looked like an older version of Shirley Jones from the Partridge family, wearing a sky-blue suit. Her hair was growing back, there was even a touch of blue in it. She seemed mentally well. Mum was looking better daily after all the years of knowing her as she once was. It was like she was a different person. She actually started looking after herself a little bit and going along to Parents Without Partners where she'd dance and mix in with society in a healthy way.

We celebrated my brother's wedding. We ate and danced. We laughed and we had a lovely day. I'd never felt so proud of my family. For some reason, my brother's wedding was incredibly special. When it came to the boys, we would all rally around. God, we loved the boys so much. I actually think they were the glue that kept us relatively together. I loved both of my brothers, and I miss them so much. If I had two wishes, one of them would be to turn the clock back to that day. I think I'd take this moment to hug them all, just once more. For a fleeting moment on that day, life seemed better. We were all together. For the first time, all of the family came together, including of the two older girls and their husbands who'd not been speaking to each other for two years. A truce happened in the car park on the day of the wedding. They all appeared to cease fire! They even said hello to me and my boyfriend. I absolutely adored him and felt much supported that day, with him by my side. I thought we'd be together forever, but he wasn't so sure of me. He was older and had years of experience with women. I was a girl, starry eyed and extremely naïve.

Boys want to spread themselves around: well, most do at eighteen. It's a stupid analogy, sowing wild seeds. He did this for years. It took many tears and much maturity to understand I was an idealist with my views on relationships. It took years to realise some of these ironclad ideas needed to be challenged, and often. Most of my ideas came from looking at others' lives. Yes, as they say, all that glitters is not gold. I adored my older sisters with their stunning looks, handsome husbands, and comfortable homes. What I didn't comprehend was that we don't always settle with a partner suited to travel through life with us, or one that is compatible. The one thing I can comment on is coming from a distorted view of relationships or trauma; it's important to be aware that it's easier to settle with another old and comfortable pattern. It takes many years and lots of counselling to become aware and see our patterns. Often, it all ends the same way. Deprivation, isolation, control, or some other form of a mistreatment. Of course, I have viewed some good relationships, and there have been a few outstanding ones. But without realising it, we move on from one relationship just to change it for the same thing with someone else.

Moving onwards, I was now working two jobs trying to support my sister and myself. She broke free and went on her own journey at fourteen. Life was totally spiralling out of control. I ended up back in Morwell with my friend's mum, Ruth, one of the sweetest ladies I knew. She asked an old school friend of hers if she would take me in as a boarder. So, I went there and after many years of being a gypsy, I was able to settle for a little time. This lady and her husband were good people. She was an extraordinary woman. A liberated woman who was always interesting. She had been the daughter of publicans and had the skills to run a hotel single-handedly. She was an attractive woman who was amusingly witty and strong. She had the gift of the gab, and I watched her handle men like they were putty in her hands. No one messed with her. And she could cook! She was the best cook I ever met, I mean, the best.

Her husband was a jolly, rotund man, and they had no kids together. His life was dedicated to the merchant navy. Fifty years of service he spent travelling to many countries. He loved the sea, still does. He would be gone for long spells at a time, and then come back with a big pay packet. Then, off he'd go again. A very kind-natured man too, who loved to eat.

Bonnie was very significant in shaping a part of the woman that I am today. Upon moving from the many places, both her and her husband said I was always welcome to return if I got stuck. As it happened, when I was around nineteen, I did just that. I became extremely worried I might end up with schizophrenia like my mother, as I'd recently had a very big loss in my life. My first time of becoming a mother came with much heartache and plenty of shame. I was eighteen when, on 2 December 1980, I gave birth to my first-born. At this stage, I was with my mum again, and as usual she was not well and at many times during this pregnancy, she would walk behind me in an undignified way. I was so self-conscious of my situation.

I woke up with this bang in my pelvic area, like an internal kick, and being so young I had no idea what had taken place, not until I called the doctor. My water had broken. With this, I walked to the phone box and called my doctor and explained what had happened, and he said to get straight to the hospital. While at the phone box, I called someone I trusted. Ruth, my friend's mother, came to me within five minutes. I was just going to walk to the local hospital. I would say the contractions started within minutes after her getting me to the hospital. No turning back now. This is a situation you can never avoid or escape.

It is very hard for me to talk about this epic event in my life for two reasons. Much shame came with this pregnancy and the birth. I was not a rough girl. Stupid and extremely dumb and naive was more the case. Then what followed was not the time I had hoped for. My life was never going to be the same again.

The Matron of the hospital asked as I went into full labour if she could stay and hold my hand. By Easter Sunday of the following year, my beautiful baby had died of SIDS. Now I was facing so much trauma it felt like I was being washed out to sea, and then as the tide came in, I was being washed up on the beach. The iceberg of trauma accumulated over my life was already greater than my ability to cope with it. I was a continual pattern of flotsam and jetsam. This nomadic young me was not yet a woman, and I was already a worn-out mess. I was barely keeping my head above water, working a day and night job at Coles, packing shelves and working checkout to make ends meet. I had no time to grieve or mourn my huge loss, and when I came home one day to my flatmate, overdosed and laying on the floor, I think it sent me over the edge, or close to it.

Of course, I called the ambulance, and being a responsible friend, told her mum about her drug issues. When her parents collected her from the hospital, they took her home to theirs and so my accommodation with her ended. Years later, and a mother herself, my old flatmate actually died from an overdose. I landed back at Bonnie and Jack's, who by now were my pseudo-foster parents. I was a bag of nerves, and super distressed, to put it lightly. My mind wasn't settling, and I became very worried about my future. Bonnie, being the pragmatic woman that she was, packed me into her car and took me off to a psychiatrist. She advised him of my losses and my concerns. 'Tell this girl that she will never be unwell with schizophrenia,' she said to him.

He asked what my mother's name was and it turned out he'd actually treated her at some point in his career. He talked to me a lot about schizophrenia and advised me that Mum's illness was not hereditary. His advice for me was to find some stability.

'Stick to the same job, and the same house,' he said. 'No moving around. Stay put!'

Which is easy to say when you have somewhere secure to live. Good old Bonnie, though. Like a responsible parent, she told me to stay with them for a little longer. I did, until I met my husband. I can now see why I said yes when he asked me to marry him. My life had been a constant struggle and I needed a stable landing. I longed for one. Jack gave me away on my wedding day, but years later, Jack and Bonnie separated. I guess it was too hard for them sustaining a marriage when you're continuously waving goodbye. I loved them both. When I was pregnant with my daughter, Jessica, I asked Jack if he fancied becoming a pseudo grandfather. His face lit up. He's been a very devoted and loving grandad to both my two children. Grandad Jack passed away august 2022 at 92. He had been a huge part my life, and my kids lives. We loved him dearly. Sadly, Bonnie passed away in 2005, a year after my own mother. Still, I'm eternally grateful to have taken so many positive attributes from this strong woman, and for all she was to me. Both firm and fair, she taught me so much, and I will always love her. She lives on in my heart as the Mother Archetype.

Ever after

Marrying my children's father was, I thought, a very positive decision. He was caring and came from a good, stable family. He was pretty calm, well-educated and there was so much I truly loved about him. He was my world. We seemed well matched, and I thought we had a very good foundation to build our lives upon. In all truth, I was looking for that place to rest, some true security, a fresh start. I wanted to be truly loved. Like in the movies, I guess. I adored him. I do believe he loved me, but he loved money more. The longer we were together, the stronger the focus became on dollar signs. I can understand the pressure money creates on young, growing families; it's tough after having children, and it can often feel like living in a pressure cooker, particularly if you don't have the necessary support. Sadly, my husband put money before anyone or anything. They say money can be a great servant, but a very poor master. From the outside we looked like the perfect couple, the stereotypical cliché.

My joy came from my kids and hanging out in the garden. Even this situation became controlled as he would tell me the backyard was his domain and the front yard mine. At least something was mine. I planted all types of flowers. I was allotted the front yard to care for, to weed, and mow. The backyard was my husband's domain. Other than my gorgeous chickens and their coop, I couldn't touch anything else. I was allowed to plant a few plants around the clothesline. I had a beautiful brown *Boronia megastigma* welcoming spring with a simple but seductive scented pleasure. Simplicity was my joy. I had a lemon-scented broom (*Cytisus*, family *Fabaceae*). When hanging out clothes, the fragrance would sweep me away. It was stunning. There was a big weeping willow. I would sing this really old song about a weeping willow.

My front yard was adorned with every seasonal flower or cutting I could get my hands on. I have photographs of my two children standing in front of my proud nurtured blooms. My kids were so little and dressed in matching sailor outfits. All my joy came from my children's happiness and the garden. The hen house was cleaned weekly, and we had fresh eggs. When a hen died, I would cry as they were part of my family. With no real education, my work was all menial jobs. Cleaning and kitchen work. All boring, but they helped to bring in extra dollars to purchase the kids extras things or pay bills.

I was doing my best to contribute and found myself working just as hard with one baby off my hip and another on the way. The list of menial jobs was a continual cycle of my existence and a time of endurance. I was always worried about money, because he would give me a royal roasting over the most ridiculous things. When my son was five weeks old, I went back to working nights in a local hotel in the kitchen. I kept trying to keep the peace, but it was useless. Resentments and bitterness had already started to build, and I was often down on myself. Attachments need to be built on trust. Our issues around finances and my husband's need to control me grew. I was struggling to make ends meet with his frugal mannerisms. He would do cash jobs as a qualified tradesman, but then, he would hide the money in places or under our wardrobe. Things took a bad turn during the pregnancy of our boy. He decided to just push me away. I felt very alone during this pregnancy. Often emotional abusers use times when a woman are at their most vulnerable to emotionally disconnect. He seemed to be working away frequently or drinking with his work mates. Still, I was trying to just keep going and do my best. Nothing much changed after Matthew was born. He was still working away and then doing extra cash jobs. When Matthew turned one, I kept thinking of my high school teacher, Mr Blaire. He was a great role model. He was the only teacher who I felt ever believed in me. I could hear his words saying that I was too young to leave school, and that a good education could take you places.

Most of my education didn't come from schooling. My education had been learnt through living life. I'm a big believer in education and finding something that sparks your interest. I believe this can lead to bigger and exciting new pathways of learning. I absolutely love to learn and have a keen enthusiasm to do so.

As a young mum in her early twenties, who'd left school at fourteen to work in a shoe factory, I needed to feel I was living for something more than the relentless task of laundry, feeding, and working hard for a small amount of dough. Somewhere between washing nappies and the dishes, I realised Mr Blaire's wisdom was right. He used to say over and over, 'Life is tough without an education!'

Mr Blaire always made me feel smart, and I think the inspiration for me to focus on getting an education began because of my ruminating on how he treated me. None of the girls I went to school with were encouraged to chase a career. The Latrobe Valley was more about industry and hard manual work for both the sexes. Yet, men were always paid more than woman. This encouragement made me believe I could be educated, although, I knew it wouldn't be easy. I would have to take micro steps. He made me believe I could be educated. Although, I knew it wouldn't be easy, I was up for the challenge. I wanted to prove to myself that I could do it.

In fact, at times, I imagined it near impossible. I was one of those restless kids. The fidgeting, nervous kid in the class, the one, that these days might be boxed into the category of having ADHD or mild dyslexia. I never read books. In fact, I was around thirty-two years old when I read my first book. Nowadays, children are provided with support, funding, and possibly a teacher's aide. There was no such thing at the orphanage. Often going to chapel was forced upon us, although I always gained pleasure from listening to the stories. Even the gospels would captivate me.

When things became tough in my marriage, I faced my fears of going 'back to school' and began to imagine I could do it. I'd always had a wild imagination and a will to get things done. Once I set my mind to believing I could, regardless of the damage I encountered throughout my childhood and youth, nothing was going to stop me. I would do what I'd always done and find ways to cope and new ways to learn. If I was to go back to school, I'd have to put my tenacious, creative brain to work. Simple. So, I attended night school. I went to TAFE and did a small refresher class on year 10 Maths and English. Passing might've looked like a miniscule step, but to be able to achieve in these subjects was a milestone for me. This gave me the confidence to study further. In 1993 I attempted my VCE as a mature student. This was in Perth, and I studied alongside many new migrants and refugees. We all got on well. The exchange of food was delectable along with conversation around the refugees' journeys to Australia. Finally, amongst these foreigners I felt I was getting somewhere. I finally felt my input was important. I'd always been able to speak well, and engage, and I liked helping others. There were many words the new migrants struggled with, especially Australian colloquialisms, and they appreciated my help. My advantage was that studying within this lovely cultural group of people was enough to propel me forward.

Getting my license was also a big milestone as this meant I could get everywhere without help from my husband, or public transport. I was twenty-four years old when I got my license and my first car. It was an old white Mazda 629 and I paid one thousand dollars for her. She was an old beauty, but in the end the petrol fumes were a concern as both my kids had asthma. It took me about a year to scrimp and save, and then I traded the old Mazda with the same salesman and car yard. I asked for one thousand dollars trade in.

'You won't get it,' my husband said.

I wouldn't budge, so the man agreed. Then, I added my savings of two thousand dollars and ended up with a nice red

Holden Gemini. It was a great little car and safe enough to transport my kids around with no more second-hand fumes. It felt good to be making a few more decisions other than domestic duties and work-related decisions.

I was slowly building myself up again. Which was another reason why hearing and believing that voice of my old teacher was integral to making some positive and intentional changes for the better. Often, we women give our power and control over to our husbands, and we can lose ourselves in a committed relationship. I'd become rather invisible and was often treated like I was stupid. I beat myself up and was self-loathing at times. My husband would give me one hundred dollars allowance each week and I had to keep a ledger to show what I'd spent the money on. Usually, the amount was spent on food, paying bills, or any other needs for the kids. I had no sense of what my husband earnt. My withdrawal slip was given to me weekly, and I went to the bank and signed by my husband to collect the much-needed funds. I started an account at the local chemist for the kids, and an account at the shoe shop for my little ones' shoes. Both of my children had inherited my turned in ankles and needed strong Clarke's boots for their developing feet. I had a very badly turned in leg as an infant and had a Popsicle stick attached to it, which straightened it out, eventually. My planning ahead was a necessity for everybody's needs to be met. And as a young mum, I kept myself last on the selfcare list. What a martyr I had become, still trying to jump to another's tune.

During the marriage, there were other little abuses that accumulated, other hairline fractures that, in the end, fractured the relationship. Love is just not enough. Looking back, we both had learnt things from our families. He had a thing for money and wealth. I needed to feel that emotional love. It just was not a good match in the end. When I hear people talk about the five different love languages, I think that none of these matter unless you can work together and have a close moral cord. I think it's important to discuss how important wealth is to you. Is your family more important? That was perhaps not even an equal situation at times.

I thank him for our children and for teaching me some good strategies around finance. Marriages end and again I felt in many ways I was responsible. My emotions were running out the door. I felt suppressed and unloved, because all his energy was heading in one direction. Disassociated was a coping mechanism. I had left the building in my head. There is never a pleasant way for a relationship to end. For years, I held myself responsible because I thought I'd sabotaged this union. I believed it was my actions that caused my two children to not have a father in their lives. In the end, I think it was obvious what was important to him and what was not. He would not engage with them when they were little. His greed and need for money made him lie to the child support agency. His new partner, who he met a few months later, turned out to be rather complicated, and she added her own insecurities to the mix.

I made it clear that the kids needed their father in their lives. It was payback. No calls to his children, no financial support for schoolbooks, his every cent was invested into properties. Greed was his ruler, and the kids were at the end of his moral list. Our son was super active just like me. He had allergies, and his father was not keen to care for him. He said he could not cope. I did it mostly for fifteen years on my own. It takes two to tango, and I tangoed alone usually in the kitchen. The trauma of childhood played a big part in my responses, my sensitivities, my anger, and my emotions as I disengaged from him. His control of me did the opposite, and it was comfortable to revolt. Most importantly, it was unhealthy and what people saw on the outside was very different to life on the inside. After the separation, I had a single mother's pension of three hundred dollars one week and two hundred and twenty dollars the following week. It truly was more money than I'd had in years, and I felt liberated. I remember taking the kids into Perth CBD and buying them some clothes and a Christmas decoration each. My daughter chose a Ferris wheel horse, and my son, a train. They were expensive items back then and were very pretty, being made of a pearly material. I even chose something for myself: a lovely jug and sugar set with little purple flowers on them. I'd always loved nice crockery; yet, I'd never had much money to enjoy anything nice and new. I didn't write those purchases in the ledger. In fact, I threw that ledger in the bin. To this day, I still use the jug and sugar set, and I still feel liberated every time it comes out of the cupboard. It also reminds me of so much financial and other deprivation. These days, that type of inter-family behaviour is called family violence.

It was hard for me to create healthy connections with someone else. This was because of my childhood and some of the people that I had trusted letting me down. We all want to feel much-loved by that special someone. For my own emotional wellbeing, I just needed to collect myself and give these dreams up. Loving that significant other isn't as important as loving myself. I was somehow subconsciously repeating my past connection with my emotionally unattainable Mum. A few years ago, I made an informed decision to have respectful, kind friendships and leave the plastic, non-obtainable romance, or hurtful relationships in the past. In saying this, there are a few relationships that stand out as life changing. I'm thankful my kids' father who taught me to budget, and I taught myself to be sensible with money. One thing I know about myself is that my generosity of spirit will never change. I am not that person who sits back wanting others to pick up the tab. I like to keep a glass half-full attitude.

I admit my life became richer after letting someone get close to my prickly echidna quills. I think the echidna represents my inner self because it is often easier for me to push away someone before they push me away first. Trauma can make us love too much, or be scared of getting close. I don't know where I sat, but getting hurt seemed to be a pattern, as well as pushing back and hurting others in return. Another relationship taught me to have fun. After so much deprivation of spirit, I found myself soaring over Mount Buffalo in a microlight, and riding on the back of a dirt bike. It was reckless fun. It was often a way to motivate some sleeping part of me. This man's bluntness inspired me to improve my writing skills. He had beautiful handwriting. In the mid-1990s, we were all still using snail mail as a form of communication. The letters I received from him were from all over the world. I was always so happy to collect one of his beautifully written letters from the local general store. Snail mail was the best, better than any email or Facebook message.

Many years later, another connection sparked my interest in reading, and other expansions of academia. My friend had come from a background of opulence and was well-read, travelled, and educated. He was tall and handsome and quite the enigma. He had been an exceptional artist with an artist's temperament. He was hard to gauge, temperamental, and abstract. We have remained friends. I enjoyed his stories of his life when he returned from overseas. We often had much to catch up on. There is a mutual respect between us, faraway from too much emotion.

I can only speak for myself, but there is enjoyment in each other's company, and it feels like a really safe connection built on trust and honesty. With maturity, I've recognised the importance of looking back and forwards with a sense of grace and gratefulness for my life.

We can always learn to forgive, and we can also say sorry for our own poor behaviours or bad deeds. As Jackson Browne sings in 'These Days', 'don't confront me with my failures, I have not forgotten them.' Many years ago someone made a disc up for me. I played it in my car and this song resonated with my heart so suddenly that, I think when I realised, my heart was more than broken. I had nothing left to give. It was a clarifying moment. How all of my past trauma had just worn me down. I threw in the towel. Life still isn't easy, but it's much more manageable.

Attachments have been really difficult for me. If anything, it was just another issue to deal with when I already felt pretty worn out and not able to cope. I tried things, but they never really worked out. For myself, at this moment, my life is very simplistic, and I really haven't bothered to meet anyone for a long time now. Relationships for me just tend to disappoint or usually add another layer of hurt. It's really hard to make yourself vulnerable. With my new grandson, I'm truly hoping to be an organic creative influence to devote some time to spending time with him, teaching him about nature and fun stuff. Maybe dreams can come true? He is beautiful and he is a new seed for a positive future. There are so many things I enjoy about the plainness of my life. So, for this time, my dance card is empty, and it's a choice I have made because my life is full, rich and happy. Sure, I get lonely at times, and I just sit with the loneliness until it passes.

Part Four

Adult Reflections

Earth angels

There is no person I take for granted. I call my friends my Earth Angels. These friendships have sustained my soul and filled it with love and joy. These beautiful friends have let me into their lives, and this is the most special gift, one that's not written on a Hallmark card. In friendship, actions speak louder than words. I thank all of my friends from the bottom of my heart. They know who they are. I have laughed and cried with them all. Often, at the same time. Boy, we have laughed through some of my darkest times. We have cried through the smallest of losses to the loss of life, the loss of a son, a brother, and a mother. Anyone who knows me well, knows I have a wicked sense of humor and a good laugh is cathartic for my abstract mind. These friends are my little rocks, my wingless angels!

Many of them have their own funny little nicknames, or terms of endearment, for me. Molly, Tingles, Beach Bud, Mary ... the list goes on. Behind each nickname is a funny story. They've been such great friends to me. True friends are the ones you can be brutally honest with and let your guard down and also have a good belly laugh with, even at totally inappropriate times. In my life, I have used these close encounters with my Earth Angels as a window into my own self. How do they see me? Am I a good child? Am I a good teenager, a good woman, a worthy wife, a nurturing mother? I have second guessed myself my whole life, but these friendships have strengthened my view of myself. While these friendships have been wonderful, I'm not always the easiest of friends to have, due to my past. There are times I've felt hurt and would simply jump ship if I felt the friendship was not a solid and safe place to be. There've been many times where I've played aloof and kept inside my shell to protect myself and avoid getting too close. This is possibly out of fear of hurt or abandonment. I have had to overcome this many times, so that I could move forward with friendships. Looking back, these friendships have sustained me through decades of hard times, laughter, and tears.

It's a two-way street. I will always be a loyal friend. If I walk away, and I have, there is a good intellectual reason why. It's better for both parties to move forward. I love my friends. I don't like friendships to be codependent or symbiotic. Its unhealthy, and I won't finance it at all. My friendships are built on respect and trust. From an early age, I was an observer.

I would gauge normality by observing my friends' families. I needed to be able to understand how families worked, and not by watching *The Brady Bunch* or *The Sullivans*. This is not a lesson you'd be able to study out of a textbook and then do an exam. Only role models or life school can teach you this. There were a few families I used as models, but there were two families who I was particularly close to. Through viewing their interactions, I saw a window into different and uniquely individual lifestyles, and my perception of belief systems was challenged. Both of these families were decent people even though they were polar opposites.

The first family consisted of a mum, a dad, and three girls. I meet them all because I became friends with one of the girls. The family was hardworking and the parents were close to their girls. At around the age of ten, I had started to spend time with this family and did so until I was in my thirties. I always hold them dear to my memories. To this day, I recognize the positive impact this family had on me, not to mention how they provided me with the opportunity to see how a family functions, normally. At the end of a hard-earned week of work, the parents relaxed and enjoyed a beer on a Friday night. Saturday morning was a time when the odd bet would be placed on the horses. My friend's father was suited to having a son, but he also had two girls. He would listen attentively to the transistor radio. Saturday night was even more chilled out. If the couple had a few too many, they might have a debate about something. All in all, they were good folk.

I think each of them had very individual, strong personalities. It's hard writing about how I, as a ten-year-old, viewed them, but I do want to say I'm forever grateful for the unique way each character in my book of life has assisted me along the way. There is a little thread of each and every one of these experiences left within me. My friend's parents had meet at a local dance in the 1950s. Apparently, her dad had a very wild youth. He had good looks and the gift of the gab. Well, that's my interpretation of him and only from the stories he told us. He was the wildest out of the brothers with the looks of an angel-faced devil. In his younger photographs, he looked like Paul Newman, with fair hair. As an older man he still had sparkly, blue eyes. The photographs on their dresser told me a story of their stunning beauty. Marg had dark hair, a big smile, red lipstick and she was quite the looker. The pair of them were well matched. Mr E had been a Bodgie, a youth culture and style in the 1950s when the boys tried to look like Elvis or any rock and roll star. The boys would wear rolled-up blue jeans with slicked back hair like a pompadour. This was the Bodgie boy type of hair style, slicked back with lots and lots of brill cream. They often wore white Bonds t-shirts or rolled up sleeves on their shirts. We all watched *Grease* with

Olivia Newton John and John Travolta, it all being about youth culture back then.

Mr E had a couple of brothers, and one sister. He and his brothers got up to all kinds of shenanigans and pranks, and I would listen to his stories with my friend. The way he told his stories was incredibly entertaining. I couldn't get enough. Hearing anyone's biographical or factual past is never boring. Ordinary people live extraordinary lives. He was my equivalent to a verbal and real-life visual experience of Albert Facey, the storyteller and author of *A Fortunate Life*. I am an auditory learner so my memory works better by listening, and Mr E's tales and yarns always kept me intrigued. One story was how he and his brother stumbled upon some TNT dynamite. They came from a coal mining town, so dynamite was a quick way of excavating. He and his brothers headed out of town in an old Holden and one by one they had turns in lighting up the sticks of TNT and throwing them out the back of the car and watching them blow. Kaboom! Most stories were just fun ones about how he enjoyed some of the travelling boxing troops and was possibly in for a round or two. He was a real character, a great storyteller, and he had a heart of gold. I liked him and, most of all, I trusted him. He was a decent person, that's for sure.

After one too many beers, he would chat and a couple of times, I noticed he become upset. My friend told me he wanted to tell this one story but became emotional and never finished it. It was a very sad story indeed. As least I think it was, don't quote me, as this was like forty-five years ago, and I heard this re-told. Some time in his twenties, Mr E had been driving along his country road not far from where he lived. It was nighttime and very dark in winter when he accidentally ran over something. There was a thud. Apparently, he had no idea what had occurred. Then, suddenly, out of the blue, a car door was open in the vehicle in front of him from where a small child fell. It's possible, he ran straight over the infant, which lead to an unfortunate and tragic fatality. Cars were not equipped with seat belts in the 1940s, 1950s or 1960s. It was a freak accident. If it were true, the harrowing effects never left this man. He was a good man with a good heart who must've struggled with this awful tragedy.

Mrs E was an outspoken and liberal woman. She did not suffer fools and she had a Scottish background, just like her husband. You just knew to not cross her. She was straight down the line and she assisted me to get my very first job. I also liked her quite a lot. She taught me how to cook rabbit stew. She really loved her golf and Saint Andrews. Scotland is the birthplace of golf. She embraced her Scottish love of the game.

Mr E enjoyed fishing and ferreting. The eldest son was great to his dad. I really liked him. He was level-headed and easy to talk to. He was into all the stuff his dad was into: fishing, rabbiting, collecting mussels and shellfish. He was a great sport. Genetically, it was innate in him to love all the things his dad loved. I was closer to the middle sister, and she was a loyal friend with a heart of gold. Again, genetics speak. She had fists on her that were as big as any on a man, and she was not at all scared to use them. With her around, I never felt scared. For the first time in my life, I just knew she'd impart fear into any bullies that were going to be a potential threat. She had no fear at all. Even the toughest girls feared her. And yet, she was soft and funny deep down, a good loyal friend.

My little sister, Jane, hung out with her youngest sister who was born premature, and I gather had a very mild intellectual disability. She was a sweet, little girl. I loved her. All three girls had unique qualities and were all extremely different from each other. They all had chores to do and they did them without question. Mum was hard; Dad a softy. If my friend had to take care of the animals, the task included being in charge of feeding the ferrets. Warm bread and milk were always on the menu in the winter, and then other meat types of food. Believe me, I was petrified of those critters with their razor-sharp teeth and avoided them as much as I could. My friend got a great belly laugh from my fear of them. The ferrets were good hunters, apparently. They would take these carnivorous, flesh-eating creatures out to the bush in small wooden boxes. Snowy was the best hunter. She'd get the smell of the rabbits and chase them out of their safe, warm warrens. I never went along, never! It wasn't a thing I wanted to see. The unwilling rabbits did end up in a big boiling pot with onions and potatoes. Mrs E's infamous rabbit stew. I'm a hypocrite as I actually enjoyed Mrs E's rabbit stew, and also her roasted rabbit.

At times, she was hard on my friend who was often left to care for her younger sister, much like myself, and I of course thought this was a lot to expect of a twelve-year-old girl. I watched my friend as she was made responsible for her younger, disabled sibling and I could empathize, understanding that pressure as I had to look after Salvation Jane. She would have to deal with her mum if she stepped out of line. The funny thing was, and I hadn't realised this until now, that I was in way over my head, caring for my little sister, with a mother who not only had mental health issues but gynecological issues and was often in bed due to hemorrhaging. As a youngster, I didn't have time to look back, I just kept moving forward and surviving, mostly by trying to keep away from Mum's outbursts and things that would set her off into a ranting, abusive rage. I think, possibly, Mum was relieved to be rid of me as much as I was to be gone from under her feet. And, if that meant taking my little sister along, I'd just take her. Consequently, both of us spent time at the house over the road with my friend and her family. They knew when I was in trouble, as Mum would scream like a banshee at the top of her lungs, calling me the most repugnant names. At times, I wished I could just crawl under a big rock like a crab, as I believed they all knew that my own mother found me hideous.

All children just want to feel loved and nurtured. Hanging with my friend and their family was better than being at my house with my angry Mum. Their house had a unique smell. It wasn't one I liked or disliked, I think it was possibly the smell of cigarettes and, on the weekend, alcohol.

On a Sunday, Mrs E always wore a dress and lipstick and looked extra nice. They always cooked a roast for a hot lunch, and Mr E's elderly parents religiously came to enjoy the roast dinner. His parents were Catholic and came after Sunday mass. Mr E's father was a tall lean man, a real gentle person. He had served in WWII and survived. His mother was short in stature, her height, possibly four foot two. She was a very little woman who loved her grandkids, and they loved and respected her. My friend's grandparents were both very caring and devoted. They always smiled. They were the salt of the earth and lovely country folk. Not often, but sometimes, the grandfather would enjoy one or two ales with his son, and a natter about the football, the horse track, or current affairs. Many times, I was invited for lunch and we girls would sit at a makeshift table, which was usually the coffee table. Over the years, I became part of the furniture and eventually all the extended family, uncle and aunties, cousins, knew me. I had been taken into the fold and everyone would acknowledge me and be open to conversation. This sounds like it's not much of a big deal; however, it was the first time I was acknowledged as a real person. My mother was abusive. Trying to fit in at home was a task, whereas fitting in there was seamless and easy, as long as I adhered to my friend's house rules, which I always did.

The boneyard

There's an old analogy about each one of us human beings having our own skeletons in the closest. Imagine the impact of so many bones, layer upon layer, piling up like a huge ancient bombora in the back closet of one's soul. The fact is that, even after generations of time have passed, the lies still resurface. Lies have an undesirable way of affecting the innocent, as one lie seeps into another and another until, eventually, they all mesh together. I have been systemically working through my own generational turmoil in this present life. The hiding of the truth has been dancing around me like the flicker of a spark just about to take off in a tinderbox. Decades before I was ever born, I was left with a boneyard full of family discrepancies to deal with. I became aware of secrecy when Mum's mother, my Nana, was staying with us because her home had been sold. I believe she had entrusted my brother-in-law to assist with this. Her belief was that men were to make the big decisions in life. Sadly for her, and many women, I would certainly disagree. I wear the pants and the dresses in my house.

One day, when I was about ten, Nana handed me a box of matches and a small suitcase with something in it. 'Burn everything,' she said.

Curious, I snuck into the bathroom while she wasn't looking and had a look at what was in the suitcase. In my hands were very old sepia photographs of people in long Victorian dresses and top hats. There were also photos of horses and other interesting things of that time. The strange thing is that I love the smell of sulphur just after you strike a match, but on this day I just stood there with the suitcase full of old photographs not wanting to do this job for her. I'd never liked my Nana, or felt close to her, yet she entrusted me with a job! A dirty one, at that.

Under great duress, I did the deed while Nana stood on the back step looking down on me. The fire engulfed each and every one of her original snapshots of the past, of that place and time in history. Mum's ancestors and mine were going up in smoke, even though I'd been reminded on numerous occasions that I was on the outside, a non-relation. Nana couldn't change a person's genetics, whether she liked it or not. I was her daughter's child. I often wondered if she had given up the ghost a little by this time; with her little cottage gone it seemed like such a sad, desperate thing to want me to do. Or was she just super organised and taking care of business, leaving no stone unturned? Was she planning her own advanced care directive? I will never know as secrecy was what she wanted on this day. I wanted to save the photos, but I was powerless. The past went up in a big plume of toxic smoke leaving a pile of ash that, eventually, was rained on or swept away with the wind like some kind of cremation. Her secrets were to remain with her. In retrospect, with the wisdom of adulthood and the yearning for a real family, I realised Nana kept her memories concealed, taking them to her grave.

The saddest secret was the night when my uncles lay on the highway, left dead or dying all those years ago. Someone kept a terrible secret, maybe even made a pact and told a lie. Whoever they were, they did not care as they drove off leaving three men for dead, leaving my mother and her parents and other close friends shattered.

In this small, gossiping town, this was a crime worthy of manslaughter charges, yet it was written off by the coroner and police. My belief is the driver took six lives that night and, in a very small community, the lies were taken to people's graves, too. To this day, no one's ever admitted to this crime. It is a serious crime to leave the scene of a road accident. It made me wonder if it were someone powerful, someone who lived just out of town heading in the opposite direction.

Someone with much to lose if they came forward, someone political, perhaps?

I hate lies. The truth hurts, but lies destroy anything good. When Mum's first love, her husband, went off to fight in the war, the army lied. They said he would come home a hero. Men of bravery don't beat their wives, frighten their children, and then abandon their family. Then, there was the biggest lie of all, one that has taken me fifty-six years to get some clarity on. Who was my father? Why did Mum not tell me the truth? I have many theories about how I came about. I'd like to live in a fantasy world and say the Calabrian saw Mum as a beautiful woman when he was living in the small cottage bungalow in the 1950s at the side of my Nana's house.

After the DNA tests came back from both the Canadian and Australian testing sites, the results were the same: a 99.6% DNA match. Throughout the next few months, I began to communicate more with my brother. I wanted to meet my biological father as soon as possible, but my brother wasn't so sure. My father was elderly and, rightly so, he didn't want to cause too much stress for his dad. He said he would deal with it, but after some time of feeling that my need to meet my father was being brushed aside, I decided to send him a large envelope of information, including, photos, letters from the orphanage, and other items in the hope of jogging his memory. It turned out he did remember Mum.

My mother's biggest thorn was her own mother. Nana was continually writing to the nuns and Christian Brothers, always interfering. When she died, she left her estate to two of her granddaughters. I found this difficult to accept as she picked two granddaughters over her own living daughter, Mum. In my estimation, I found Nana a very strange woman indeed, considering she had one living daughter who desperately needed help. She had eight grandchildren, not two, and she had great grandchildren. It actually showed the biases she had all along. How does someone leave a legacy that continues to tear the family apart? I am baffled by such bitterness. Imagine if Nana had left her little cottage to Mum. The boys would've come home as that was always the issue with the Catholic authorities, not to mention how Mum was struggling for help and some stability. Nana simply had no generosity of spirit, and this kind of behaviour has been passed unconsciously through the generations. This one time, I remember being at one sister's house. All of the her kids were sitting at the big dining table, a makeshift table, having lunch. Jane and I were chatting when Nana looked straight at my face and told me, 'Little piggies should be seen and not heard.' This was my own Nana. I shuddered.

As a grandmother myself, I would never speak to my grandson like this. He's a beautiful child who I dote on. I adore him and his sweet little perfect self. Another time,

Nana couldn't help but undermine my singing aspirations. I'd been watching Nelson Eddy and Janet McDonald in an old black-and-white movie where they'd done a duet, an Indian love call. I decided, loving music the way I did, that I might actually become a famous opera singer, or, even a singer. On this particular day, I went outside and belted out some tunes to my old cat, Smokey. He seemed to really like it. I'm not sure why Nana was even there as she never chatted or talked much with Mum. Maybe it was to do with Mum's little inheritance from her father's side. Anyhow, I thought as Nana was there, why not belt out a tune and see what she thought about my potential musical career. She looked at me quite distastefully as if disgusted with my attempt at singing.

'Oh,' Nana said. 'Who stood on the cat's tail? You'll never be a singer!'

To this day, I still laugh. If Nana had passed any words of encouragement from her mouth, it would've contaminated my already congruent young thoughts about the bitter, twisted, old woman. The only nice gesture Nana gave us was the day when we were leaving Traralgon and you could see her cottage from the train. She waved us off with a mop or a handkerchief.

'Wave back to Nana,' Mum said to Jane and me.

We did as we were told.

The relationship I had with my family was difficult, but

most difficult was the one I had with Mum. I loved my Mum, regardless of her behavior, and yet, I often felt she disliked me. Mum and I had a tumultuous relationship. Was it because of how I was conceived? Was it just a reflection of Mum's relationship with her own Mum? Was it Mum's mental health, or simply a combination of all factors?

No ordinary moments

To this day, I feel grateful for the sanctuaries and havens that I was able to find friendship and acceptance in. If it wasn't for some of the incredible synchronicities where I stumbled upon great people along the way, I honestly don't know if I'd still be alive today. At times, it was the generosity and kindness of others who made me keep going. With them, I no longer felt alone and felt that I could get through anything. I was a survivor. I still am. I will be eternally grateful for the second family who took me in, and who kind of stumbled upon me too.

One day, I was going for one of my long walks with my little sister. We were a couple of miles out of town, as I had a habit of always trying to head away from the houses and into a bush somewhere. Exploring like Matthew Flinders trying to find places that no man had already found. I believe I may have found a few unnoticed pockets of native bushland. So, this one time, this lady pulled up in a mint green Valiant and asked what we were doing so far out of town.

'Going for a walk,' I replied.

I noticed a girl sitting next to her who was a little older, and taller, than myself. She offered us a ride. Because I considered myself street wise, I accessed the situation. A mother and daughter ticked the safety boxes, so in we hopped. After that, I kept running into this girl as she worked at the local fish and chip shop. We became great friends, and her family was warm and sociable. They had a sweet little fluffy dog called Buffy. He had the run of the front yard while the mother watered the front garden. He was a Maltese cross and was the cutest fluff ball. He was always groomed by his owner and never unkempt. They also had a chinchilla cat lazing around calmly on the porch. My friend's mum loved birds. They had a budgie displayed in his cage as you entered the closed-in porch area. I loved animals, so while knocking on the front door, I would admire him chatting away to himself, content and happy. There was also a lovely garden at the front of their home filled with roses and other flowering shrubs.

My friend's mum especially enjoyed propagating fuchsia with their different colored bells. Yes, the 1970s had challenges, and so I found comfort in simple things. I'd always noticed the details, and sometimes they'd stick in my memory. The days when a vase was used and populated with the prettiest blooms from one's garden was always a sight of beauty. My friend had a younger sister, Mary, plus two younger brothers. They were just an outstanding family. Sue had a bright green room and she seemed to like monkeys. Her sister's side of the room was covered with pictures of horses cut out of magazines. We read the latest *Dolly* magazines and loved Bay City Rollers and David Essex. There was freedom to listen to music and laugh. It was all super innocent, and on hot days we swam in their pool. Never once did I see any sign of aggression in this family, just respect and love. There was so much happiness and stability in this family. My friends became an integral part of my life. She was one of my Earth Angels.

Ruth, my friend's mother, was a real nurturer. She was gentle and warm, a loving mother, the type to cut her kids' sandwiches up in neat little triangles and wrap them in rainbow wax paper. She took such time and care with everything she did. There was only one thing I struggled to do with my friend and her mum, which was the grocery shopping. She was extremely slow at doing this. If we went shopping, I swear it would be a good three hours before we were back in the car and heading home. I was a little fidgety as a girl; patience was not a virtue of mine. Regardless, I tagged along as it was special to be invited, and besides, we girls could go from one side of the town to the other, crossing under the railway line, and looking at the shops. We would be back in time to help place the big brown shopping bags, full of groceries, in the boot of the car.

Now I had two role model families from which I could establish some template for what a functional family might look like. They were all great people with the bonus of having plenty of family around them, including cousins on both sides. Not only that, but they also interacted together in a functional way that I wasn't used to. It may sound odd, but noticing the current of general happiness in both of these families has always stuck with me. I suspect this is because my homelife was the opposite. Observing these two families was a great life lesson as I was able to work out how good people could behave. They were friendly, respectful, welcoming, and kind. There was no yelling and no abuse in their homes. I also learnt that good people usually have nice, caring friends and family around them. This was a very important life lesson to learn at a young age because it showed me how clearly different my childhood had been. I did become a part of this family's life as much as my friend's family. Both families trusted me. To be able to knock on the door and see my friends was such a wonderful experience.

When I was twelve, I was given the keys to the house of one of these friends to feed their Labrador, Goldie. She was a gentle old soul, and loving. I would go across and feed this rotund dog. She was quite the barrel. She would be so happy to see me, especially just upon feeding time. I took on the role with great pride and importance. This family trusted me with their keys, which may seem insignificant, but in my opinion, there are no ordinary moments. Never to this day have I stolen or abused anyone's trust. I was told you earn trust and once you've earned it, you should respect it like it is sacred. From spending time with good people and friends, my inner disturbances or demons were disturbing me less and less. The feelings of inadequacy were starting to leave me alone, and I was dealing less with my inner battle of feeling like an imposter. Suddenly, I was experiencing trust, and I was able to feel safe.

These families had wonderful friendships and grandparents and uncles and aunties. My own foundation became stronger, and I began to have self-esteem and confidence that I'd never experienced before. I disagree with many experts that say if you don't have love and nurture in your early years, you'll never be able to form healthy attachments like children from more loving, nurturing backgrounds. I was written off many times in my life by some family members, and some of my friends' parents who thought I was a runaway rebel. I was the one least likely to succeed. But I've succeeded and I ended up finding role models and nurturing a decade later than the usual. That's been my normal. Sure enough, I live with anxieties and keep away from triggers. I have been privy to others that have similar issues due to lesser life experiences than my own. Labelling is easier than looking at individual journeys.

Strength and resilience are such important attributes. I have read so many autobiographies and find it captivating and inspiring how people handle life so uniquely. The one thing we all have in common is our remarkable story of resilience.

My life has been and will continue to remain a beautiful tapestry of individual threads weaved by people. It is made up of happy, warm autumn colours, but also darker shades, thus pushing me to leave a legacy of forgiveness where unkindness and judgements were made by others towards me along my life's path. I am thankful for these dark shades. They assisted me to strengthen areas of weaknesses, to toughen me up, and enable me to build the resilience needed to help my soft character become strong. I'm often misunderstood. I would describe my personality as a little aloof, or comfortable and at ease. I have a quirky and inventive mind. This creativity has often kept my mind active and provided me with a form of protecting myself at times from the damage that could've scared my malleable young self even more. My life wasn't easy. This is true, but I also think we are given no more than what we can handle, which is why I'm very grateful I was blessed with a jovial disposition. Without this, I never could've lasted the years of trauma I encountered. I might've taken every moment of my life seriously, and then where would I be? Maybe in the end I laughed myself through all of the awkward and difficult situations by deflecting and clowning around.

Years later, in community services and operating as a mental health practitioner, I swear I got through many serious situations by adding my own sense of humour into the mix. This way of thinking has assisted me to make light of many things and events that have not only been so painful, but also at times confronting. My colleagues were also happy to partake in the odd office shenanigan with me. When they read this they will know exactly what I'm talking about. We never were disrespectful to our clients. Never. I'm a huge advocate for the respect and ongoing support for the most vulnerable within our community. They face so much adversity, and I've meet wonderful people in my career and listened to the journeys of others. Recovery was always my focus when working with my clients and 'to do myself completely out of a job.' Meeting this lofty objective means I've achieved my goal and assisted someone to move forward and upward so they can live empowered and free lives, and make their own decisions.

Woodshedding

Life experiences can hinder our thoughts and behaviours only if we let the past keep having control over the now. To be candid and open to honesty is important to me. I realised that no one in the end is to blame. And that we, the adults, need to take responsibility for our behaviours and outcomes as we get older. There is no use blaming our parents for what we need to deal with ourselves as adults. There are disappointments and some very titanic losses, but we should be able to take charge and utilize tools, such as therapy counselling, to help us move forward. I have experienced breakdowns, or breakthroughs in my life. Just recently, actually, while devoted to write this book, I was struggling for three months. Covid and the lockdowns in Victoria tapped into the trauma of institutional life. We were trapped in a big, awful building and although there were many of us, we were all alone.

Living alone was fine like it is now; feeling so disempowered was extremely unhealthy for someone with my background and past, I started to notice a few more chinks in my armour. I had many of my triggers going off. I was going to be shut away from my family, my son, and my grandson. My daughter in WA. I was in total panic, fright-flight mode. This broke my heart as my grandson was tiny, born in December 2018. The Premier shut us within five kilometres of our homes. They were close to Port Melbourne, and then he made the Mornington Peninsula part of the broader Melbourne catchment area, of course. Anyone who lives on the Peninsula knows that all the wealthy have properties in our area. They travel from Toorak down and always have. One of the worst years in my life was 2020. It ended up being a great year too, as the resilience kicked in. I had just purchased my home; I was building a rose garden and writing this book. I had to adapt and adjust quickly. All my usual coping mechanisms were gone: yoga, physio, friends, family. I had a parttime job, and to make this worse, it was in a big hospital.

At the start of the pandemic, people were praising the front-line staff in hospitals, sending gifts, pizzas and even perfume. When shit got real, many friendships waned, and others flourished. Families struggled, and the elderly became invisible. I remembered my son in-law, who is in the entertainment industry, taking on a job for Uber Eats. They were in Perth. The person he was delivering to clearly had no mask around, so the lady appeared with a brown paper bag with cut-out eyes. He got back in the car and relayed the story to my daughter, and they nearly wet themselves laughing. My daughter is a scientist. We believed in the pandemic. We were struck with the stupidity and conspiracies coming from the Cookers. I think the only ones that gained a lot during this time were the big drug companies, while small businesses went broke and shut down. I was on the dark side of fifty, if it was not for my daughter in WA. helping me with her kind phone calls daily. She called to check in on me and make sure I was doing okay. My good friends called me often in those worst weeks, and my counsellor set small tasks for me to get through. It was tough. Most of my friends were too far away and others that I considered to be really close were too freaked out by me working in a hospital. Let's say it was impossible with friends who became super rigid. What a nightmare it was to be dictated to by a premier, who clearly had digs on the peninsula too.

Although I'd describe myself at this time as being 'buoyant,' it was really not a great time. I was so tired and fragile, and I retreated into myself. I can look back now and say it was a hard time, which I now recognise, as I look over my whole life, was brought on by a relentless series of unfortunate events. For myself, and I can only talk about my own personal experiences, I had to put on a brave face and keep working, but I'd collapse as soon as I got home. I was not in a good space, and it was a very big battle. I actually hit the lowest of times, including having suicidal thoughts. I felt extremely disconnected from anyone and everyone. If it were not for my wee little dog, Bob, and my four little hens and my cat, Willow, I don't know what I would have done. Pets are the best company. I felt for so many living alone. I felt for the mothers in my neighbourhood trying to home school. I purposely built a small pop-up library for the mothers to collect books. Some friends disagreed with my idea, but I did it anyway.

I'm not sure how I would've coped. Loneliness is an awful time. Even when I'm not struggling, I isolate myself, so imagine during this time when I had spiralled into a complete hibernation. It's now 2023 and I still have not recovered completely from the side effects from Covid. Not the illness (I never got it) but the lockdowns. In the end, I barely spoke to many of my friends or acquaintances. My inner babble and thoughts were exhausting me. I left most of my self-battering and self-loathing for counselling sessions. I resurfaced a little stronger and I was okay. It was a tough time, woodshedding, but I came out the other end with plans to move forward. To move on. When my son rang me close to eight months later crying, he said this had had an awful effect on his mental health. They had gotten Covid. Thankfully to this day, I haven't had it. No doubt I will, and I am not concerned.

The most important love in my life is my kids. I have always felt very close to my children. They are both adults now and my son is a father himself. As a parent, I wanted little or no harm to come to my children. My aim was to always be a good parent, and I think I did the best job I could. I tried to give my children all the things I didn't have while being a single parent, working and trying to be two people all rolled into one. After leaving my husband, I used the small amount that came in the settlement of thirty thousand dollars to build a home for myself and my children. Both of them had issues with asthma, so keeping them warm was very important. I purchased a block of land for eleven thousand dollars, plus taxes. Back then the cost of a home was close to seventy thousand dollars. We had a wood fire like a Conara, and for back up, a heater that ran off two gas bottles.

One particular night, my son had been to footy training and I hadn't collected the sticks for the fire in the bush out the back of our home. I was low on gas in the bottles as I also used the gas to cook our evening meal. It seemed I was always trying to make ends meet. Still, we had what we needed, food and a roof over our heads.

On this particular night, I had my son by my side, he was about seven. I was in a rush to warm the cold cottage up.

Usually, we were home earlier, but we'd been out and we had no fuel for the dense red gum logs for the Conara wood fire. Both Matthew and I would find kindling and bunch sticks into faggots. We'd have bundles at the front door ready to get the fire going immediately. On this night, we didn't have them, and I was frazzled with no dinner cooked, a cold house, and two asthmatic kids to care for.

My mind was everywhere else other than where it should've been. Rushing and without thinking, I took the lid off the petrol can, filled it with petrol, and then heaved it into the fire. If you've ever completed fire training, you would understand what happened next. Within a second, the invisible vapour from the petrol was ablaze. It went into the can of petrol. The top of the can was suddenly alight.

I flew out the door like the Road Runner with the Coyote on my tail as I thought it was going to blow up in my face and burn Matt and the house down. None of my firemen friends will believe this. My heart near popped out of my chest. When I reached the front lawn, the flame was completely gone. Vanished! Now, that is something truly unbelievable. As God as my witness, I couldn't believe it was snuffed out completely. My poor son's face was as white as a sheet. We had a great fire that night! And, we lived to see another day. A miracle occurred. I could be canonized and sainted for that. I'd need at least another two to be regarded as a saint, and I myself am not that pious or a Godly woman. I can certainly tell you, that night, I know I said 'fuck' more than once I ran out the door with the top of the petrol can alight.

How does one learn to be a good parent? I used to think it was a learnt process passed from grandparents and parents down to the next child-bearing generation. My parenting role models were totally defunct, other than observing my good friends and their families. No surprise, when under vast amounts of ongoing pressure, I displayed signs of burnout at times; if really pushed, I might yell. After this, I would beat myself up and lose sleep over anything I'd done wrong. It became clear to me that culture and tradition, good or bad, certainly is passed down through the generations. Trauma can also be generational. In my own history, I can see the differences now, three generations later. I feel that my kids are really strong and that regardless of any shortcomings I may've had, I actually did a really good job considering the loveless childhood I'd endured. Both of my kids are the most amazing adults. They are strong, resilient, clever, artsy, musical, and so much more.

They are both respectful to their partners and their new extended families. My son is a really great father, and I know he will never leave his boy. He will give him everything, and then some. My children are very loving and caring of each other. I feel I surely did some good mentoring. As mentioned, no one person is perfect. Due to never having great family bonds myself, I feared my kids might end up the same, with no sense of family or connection to their family. Their father was infrequently involved and living a new life in WA. I didn't want my children to miss out on their relationship with their grandparents, and so I headed back to Victoria after our separation. I had a courageous conversation with my mother-in-law. I call it this because I'm not one to ask for anything. But, when it came to my kids, I would walk over broken glass for them. So, we agreed the children would stay every now and again with their grandparents, as this would be beneficial and healthy, giving them a long lasting connectiveness and linking them to their family. With their dad out of the picture, it was so important that we organised a different pathway for this to take place. My in-laws agreed to this with open arms. The children visited their Oma and Opa. They were dedicated grandparents, both of them, and from this grew a very close bond. Once a month, they got a break from me and I got a chance to re-charge my batteries. These two aging grandparents were amazing, salts of the earth. Truthfully, we all have remained forever grateful for their devotion.

My grown-up kids are exceptional achievers, my daughter was always shy and as a teenager, she hid under a shell. She was quiet, but always very intelligent; both my daughter and

I acknowledge her personality is from her Dutch paternal grandfather (Opa). My son always had the gift of the gab and was cheeky and personable, and I knew that he was also able to reach many people by the way he interacted with people who instantly warmed to his personable, happy manner. Both children were very different babies, children, and then they had different challenges as youths, but they finally bonded together as adults. They are extremely close and very loyal to each other. They are musical and extremely talented when it comes to their craft. Both have performed. Matt's music was played on Triple JJJ one year which was super exciting for us all. I don't care what anyone thinks because he was definitely the best looking one on the EP cover, by far.

Both of my kids worked hard academically to set their vocational pathways and to reach their goals to a high standard. The year Matt finished his adult apprenticeship, he was listed as nominee for Apprentice of the Year. That very year, only a month or so later, he was involved in a workplace car accident, suffering a broken back, foot, and other debilitating injuries. The thing about my son is his attitude! After seeing him in pain a number of times at the Alfred Hospital in Melbourne, he was finally given a back brace to help him get up and moving. He sent me a selfie of his huge smile. This young man has the strength of a lion and a heart to match. He was a busy child, hyperactive, and he kept me always on my toes and on the move. He had this smile that was like a melting moment. It would melt anyone in a moment. He was always helpful and, when on my own, he would assist me with so many tasks. He helped me paint half of the boards on our new cottage before they went up. He was only seven years old at the time. He would wheelbarrow dirt if I was tired, and throw our dog on the top for good measure. Very strong and supportive. His learning skills were similar to my own. I would make stories up and tell him stories. He loved this and then I'd make up a few more. My next book is for my son, at his request. It will be a kid's book of the stories I told him and his sister as a child. To this day, whenever I see him with his skateboard, it reminds me of the stories I made up and told them when they were small. I haven't seen him without a skateboard in twenty-four years. I am so proud of him. He was always a go-get-it boy and teenager, and he didn't suffer fools as a man. Now, he is a father himself and is a wonderful role model for his son.

My daughter was, as a little girl, always singing and playing quietly. She was a thinker. From her early school days, she was a high achiever and she loved to draw and make cards for me. As a twelve-year-old, she went through a stage of communication via a letter under my bedroom door, and I would write back to her answering or talking about whatever the topic was. Recently, I gave her a box of personal things and these letters popped out! She was quite curt if she didn't get a response in time. Now I see her as a very unassuming achiever. She works one room away from the current PM when he is in residence in Perth. She is a scientist, with honours.

She is one of the kindest, caring, and giving daughters a mother could possibly ever want. Never does anyone's birthday or a special event occur without her giving a card or small gift to the lucky recipient. She has the heart of true warrior. Having faced many health issues, she soldiers on.

Forget me not

I have no doubt Mum tried her best at being a good mother. Having eight children by the age of forty-three was no mean feat, with her last little surprise being a glimmer of hope, Salvation Jane. Mum held onto her for dear life. The two boys, before me, were loved and embraced by all. For Nana, they were a replacement for her two sons. They had an Irish father, and he was also a Catholic. My grandmother was into the very fair, blue-eyed look, but my dark, olive skin, arriving five years after the boys, was not at all a welcome birth. Still, I have read Mum's letters to the state government and authorities, and I believe she had once bonded with me and loved me dearly. She was still breast feeding me before I was stolen away as a baby.

After the war ended, Mum experienced domestic violence at the hands of her returning veteran husband. She had so much potential, yet kept on getting knocked down. Although, she did come from good stock and a loving family, she encountered so much hardship. Having been taken out of school as a youngster due to a diphtheria epidemic, Mum did not continue her education. I believe the domestic abuse added to her already fragile mind. They say men like to enjoy what they see. Women, on the other hand, believe what they hear. Many men can fool a woman who is kindly and naive by whispering a handful of sweet nothings. Any help Mum received came from her kind father and grandmother in those early days after her husband disappeared and, eventually, went AWOL.

I've realised the system failed Mum. She encountered hardship after hardship with no support from the army, social services, or the only man she ever married. Mum could've had different outcomes, if only the times had been different. But what is the point in wanting to rewrite her life? All I can do now is focus on the special moments we had together and extract the treasures of truth, and stories that are gems to me. I remember travelling to the city on the train with Mum. She was sometimes spontaneous and would take us places. She showed us the Old Block Arcade and took us to the museum, and often to the Moe races. One day, she packed our clothes, and we went to the coast, Port Philip Bay. We visited her wealthy family in Chelsea and Hampton. This was family on her mother's side. I remember the grand piano in their home. A piano was a sign of opulence and an educated, cultured family. Mum had named me after her cousin Frances. They had bonded as children. She said Frances was a saint, so I took this as a compliment. When I think of Mum, I think about the changing faces of her character, but most of all, her stories. If I took her and the children for a picnic or a drive, she would share a little snippet of her life all of a sudden. My Mum fascinated me with stories of her life before her brothers died. She told me of the places they went and the chocolate smelling lilies out in Gormandale. She, herself, grew portulacas and violets. She told me of her father riding a bicycle into Loy Yang and Traralgon to work. She cooked delicious jam tarts and scones, and she always had a bowl of fruit or a small vase of flowers on the table. She kept a very clean home; there was no dust. It was always spotless. One thing I will never forget is when she visited us when I was a new mother. My baby Jessica was the same age I was before the authorities took me. I overheard her chatting to my infant baby daughter while looking into the wall mirror. She was clearly confused, she said, 'Finally, I got my little darling girl back!'

Had I heard correctly? What a sad and insightful thing, all in one moment. My mum had loved me. Her trauma and no contact or being able to bond with me had always made her different and so distant. At twenty-three years of age, this was a defining moment. Disease causes disease in a spiritual sense. Mum had suffered far too much. I forgave her. I was never going to deny her of being a grandparent. She became Nana, and she was always kind and giving to everyone.

Mum partially taught me how to make her famous ginger beer. Her memory was fragmented from too much electric shock treatment. She also divulged her recipe for sweet pickles. That was simple. It came from the back of the Ezy-Sauce bottle. She would catch a taxi out to Tyers. I built a cute cottage on the Walhalla Road. I would make her scones and treats. My mother was in many ways childlike. We talked about many things, especially my love for gardening. We visited Jean Galbraith's home in Tyres together. Mum loved native flowers, as I do. She knew of Jean as she was a well-known Gippsland lady and had lived there all her life. Jean was born in 1906, in March, like Mum. She was eighteen years her senior and she passed away 2 January 1999, six years after we moved to Tyers. She was an Australian botanist, gardener, writer of children's books and a poet. Her gardens were later opened by Mrs Archibald for the public to visit on weekends.

I was captivated by her. What an unassuming legacy she had left behind. She was known to travel to the Royal Women's Hospital and gift bouquets of flowers to ladies with no family. She found lots of native plants and they were named after this unassuming botanist. Jean was up there with

Edna Whaling. Mum also shared stories of Grace Coles and other well-respected identities in the small region.

The most enjoyable tale was about the heritage listed manor, Hollydale, owned by Jack and Poppy McGauran. While John Senior pursued a political career, they employed my grandparents between 1931-1933 as caretakers. Mum remembered running happily through the daffodils with her brothers at the homestead. If you know this area, this old home had daffodils sprouting every spring. Mum's family came down from Maribyrnong, Melbourne, to care for the homestead after the Great Depression. It was a very grand building. It was built by a butcher from Williamstown, Mr Grubb. My mother was around seven years old at this time. My grandfather had fought in the Great War, and he worked until he dropped because he was unable to get a war pension. The times during and after the Great Depression were tough. Mum's father had a long list of instructions that Jack McGauran left him. He was to build sheds, repair fencing, paint, and complete other works near the boathouse on their pond. He was happy to have some help from their eldest son my uncle, Sydney Wood, who was strong and only twelve years old.

The McGauran family were known to be frugal at times. This is a hearsay story from a trustworthy source, but according to the son of a local lamp oil delivery business, there were several paraffin-oil lights that led up the lengthy driveway to the homestead. Jack was known to give strict instructions to only fill the lamps nearer to the door of the large, rambling house. The poor often remained disadvantaged, as the wealthy have the power to pay or to avoid payments owing. I gather there was a hierarchy, and my grandfather possibly was seen as a poor English migrant.

When you're wealthy you have the upper hand. The McGauran family, who were influential in the Catholic Church, eventually became publicans and the owners of a local hotel in Traralgon. Mrs McGauran gave donations to the local Catholic church. Politics and religion were as influential as each other and as habitually corrupted as each other. Big Catholic families knew each other from church, or in the community.

My understanding is the McGauran family returned to the homestead around 1933-1934.

Old Jack never paid my grandfather for all his hard work. He never reimbursed him for materials or his time. Maybe he thought it a fair trade that my grandparents stayed there, free of rent. That was not the case, as labour and materials all come at a price. My grandfather never complained about the treatment by old Jack John McGauran. He, like my grandfather, was born in late 1880s and was as tough as nails and his money was his foundation to build his respect and boldness on. My grandfather died early in his life after manually working most of it into his fifties. There is a court named after him, which is situated in Traralgon called, Wood Court. Mum was the same age as John Junior, Poppy and Jack's son, and I believe they had been friends as children. They were both born in 1924, as was the boy Lennie Gwyther, who Mum also remembered.

In 1932, Lennie rode from Leongatha on his pony, Ginger Mick, all the way to Sydney to witness the opening of the Sydney Harbour Bridge. He was only nine years old at the time and the distance he travelled was over one thousand kilometres. He rode through fires and bushland and would be stopped along the way by kind strangers offering him a cool drink, food, or shelter. Indeed, Mum's long-term memory was amazing. That period from when she was about sixty to her turning seventy-nine was definitely the best. With that small window, I saw the person she had been and certainly the potential of whom she should've been if not so fraught with such trauma in her youth. This chapter is dedicated to you, dearest Mum. It took a long time for us to really bond again, possibly thirty-two years.

I know you loved me at the start and in the end. Rest in Peace, my sweet forget-me-not.

A mother's job is never done

I never really envisioned heading down the same road as Mum. Although, some scenarios often felt similar when I was alone and struggling with my two kids without any financial support, emotional help, or regular breaks. Many times, I felt I was missing a few beats. I would simply get worn out. Most of time everything was a blur and I, like an ever-ready battery, didn't get much rest. I kept working and going, crash and burn, keeping on through those years of children's illnesses and endless tasks. Now, most newly single parents are required to have parenting plans in place so that everyone has time out and the kids get to enjoy both parents. The plans are devised around the children's scholastic needs. In my solo days when the kids were young, being fatigued was awful. I was trying to work and study. All the balls were up in the air and if they fell, there was no one but me to put them back up. To never have had the luxury of proper holidays or 50/50 care was draining on my personal resources, but I managed.

One main reason for not having the division of care planned was that my husband and I lived in different states. Also, he just didn't seem to want that responsibility. These days, men want to be accountable. Back then, the system failed us all. There were two parents, yet only one was accountable. Sound familiar? Yes, this was the second generation of fatherless involvement. There is no law that could make a father take responsibility for his own children while the mother is constantly saying sorry. I'm truly sorry, but you can't have those new shoes this month. I'm truly sorry but we might not have enough money for that school camp. I'm sorry your dad sent you a gift in the post and it did not arrive. There was no replacement either. The sorry thing went on and on. I did my best to lay-buy items, and I used other forms as ways to provide for my kids. I'm sorry your dad doesn't call you weekly. There is no law than can collect funds, as in child support, from a man who evades and dodges his financial duty to his children.

Our relationship was over years before we parted, but his bitterness should never have left two vulnerable kids with a mother that at times was struggling to cope in so many ways. Even if he'd just paid the school fees straight to the school, this would've made my kids feel loved and cared for by their father. I despise the child support formula, what a total waste of time! Paying maintenance doesn't work if the person paying is creative with numbers and runs their own business. It's also super hard when they have a very good grasp on how to escape the system. Truthfully, in the end, the father just lets his kids down. Another thing you couldn't do in my day was make a man have access to his children. The family court's mediation process is fast and often a waste of everybody's time. I sat alone after travelling a vast distance to planned family mediation appointments. The children's father, who considered his paid job to be more important than planning the contact and access to his children, didn't show up. Men move on, and quickly; often they go on to have more children and leave their old lives in the dust. My husband met a new women three months after we split, which he was entitled to do. Do not get me wrong. I have friends who are exceptional fathers. My brother was one of them. Usually these friends are escaping their own domestic violence and emotional abuse. They still fight for the right to see their children. Yes, I have met men who have also been hurt as much as women. Totally devoted fathers. My friend Trevor was a single dad. He's a good family friend still to this day. We are great mates. We meet while working together in the 1980s and were reconnected after both of our marriages dissolved in the 1990s.

Financially, it was tough providing a holiday, with little or no money after Christmas, and many single parents are faced with school uniforms, books, and so much more in the coming year ahead. Entertainment during this long break was tricky, but this particular year was different. Trevor was head chef for one summer at The Esplanade Hotel in Inverloch. It had been established in 1896. In the 1990s, Inverloch was progressing and growing. It had a small township in Cape Patterson and in the surrounding areas in South Gippsland. This one particular year, Trev invited me, the kids, and our dog, Millie, to come and stay. When we arrived, I didn't know how this was going to work out. The last time I'd been to this hotel was after a surfing trip with friends. They had stopped in for a lunch while I had paid for a shower. I was always the clean freak, not unlike Mum. I hadn't been into the upstairs part of this hotel since the 1970s. Imagine my surprise when I came here to stay for this holiday and we head up the creaking, carpeted stairs behind Trevor. He opened the door on the landing and in we walked to a four-bedroom unit, complete with kitchen and all the amenities built for the publicans and their family. We were amazed. We were up so high and overlooking roof tops along the esplanade. We seriously did not pay for anything, not as much as a lemonade. My friend wouldn't allow it. He even snuck into the kitchen at night and grabbed bacon for breakfast. The kids and I were invited for counter teas while we stayed. Both my kids were excited, especially my son. As a growing, active boy, he loved his food and was always hungry. They were told to order sweets as well!

On the first night, Trevor took us on the Howard Extraordinaire Ghost Tour. With torch in hand, we ventured out into the squeaking corridors. The old hotel didn't get electricity until way after the Depression. Most hotels operated by candle, gas light, or, in the streets, by Arc lighting. Inverloch was turned on around 1934. Walhalla, not far from where we lived, only turned on the power in 1998. So away we went along creaking corridors and into the darkened rooms with one small torch being shown the peculiar hidden inner rooms within this old rustic hotel. One room, I remember, was situated above the main front doors. It had possibly been a ball room, or a room for entertaining, maybe a large dining room in its day. Being dark constantly adds to the mood, and Trevor would talk and hold the torch, and then he would touch someone. I remember letting out a scream that would've raised a few ghosts from their sleep. Here we were all gasping with our mouths open, totally enthralled, and scared out of our wits, and I would fall for it every time. He was a scallywag, always up to shenanigans. Slowly, and on edge, we crept around, and it was no surprise that Trevor had left the best till last.

The finale was a very strange room. It was situated just above the main windows and doors downstairs. There were these little beds in rows painted uniquely in colours with names painted elegantly on them. These small beds resembled the fairy-tale of *Snow White and the Seven Dwarfs*. There was some weird story that the previous post-WWII publicans had fostered children and had made each child a bed as a gift. The sentiment was that if the children ever returned, their beds would be waiting for them. Still, I found all of this very creepy at the time. My impression was they were remnants from a stage production, a pantomime.

The Esplanade was a very popular pub, and after lunch we would wait for Trev to finish cooking. On a good night, it was free drinks for Trevor and friends. They possibly drank the revenue away. During the day we would head to catch a few waves. Matt loved the surf. Usually, we packed food and headed to Eagle's Nest, closer to Cape Paterson. The water was always nice there. Later on, if Trevor didn't join us, I would go and meet my friends downstairs after the night meals had been cooked, and see how many meals they'd served up and counted for the entire day. It was gobsmacking to hear the final counts. Of course, they were all holiday patrons and not many of the locals dined in the lounge. They stuck to the general bar, as did all our friends. It was just a nice catch up and a chance to engage in grown up conversation, maybe a beverage or two. On Friday or Saturday, there was usually some really good live band playing. With our three kids safe and just above us upstairs, there was no stress or concerns. There were always plenty of snacks and a couple of videos. My daughter was close to fourteen by then. I think Trev was a bit of a binge drinker back then, not harmful, all in merriment. I was never a big drinker. Trevor was a party animal. He was a best friend and the best fun. This man was well-read, had great connections with people, the gift of the gab, and the ultimate giver of positive outcomes. Either way, we were grateful for his generosity.

Most summers we'd spent broke and local, so it was a change from just taking my kids out to the local Wirilda Pumping Station in Tyers for a dip. The summer with Trevor was so worth it just to see the kids enjoying life. He'd always been a wonderful family friend and our kids got on well. He was funny and witty and good with my two children, and a great friend to me and to my partner at the time. We were great mates. During those summers we meet lots of good people. I got so much joy and happiness from seeing my son so happy. He loved the beach. This trip was the highlight of all that summer. Only another struggling single parent would or could understand the sheer importance of this generosity! For the first time ever I didn't have to worry about a thing. The kids could have whatever they liked. This was a really big deal, as we hardly ever had takeout. We just couldn't afford such luxuries. This was like being 'Pub Royalty.' Trevor, an Earth Angel, was family, as were my ex-husband's mother and father.

They were absolutely dedicated to my two kids, and I am forever grateful for their assistance. I never insulted the grandparents by saying things were tough. I think they knew that things were strained. It was hard for my kids because their father lacked the ability to physically communicate with them. He sent a letter to his mother to pass on to his own kids the news of the birth of the baby he was having with his new partner. With each new birth, my kids felt further and further displaced. I watched their little hearts ache. I remember my son saying now we will be pushed even more away. The sufferers caught in the middle of separation are always the children.

At times during those teenage years, and I think other parents would agree, it can get tough. There were times I didn't like being a parent on my own. Overwhelming comes to mind, especially as they got older. No matter what decision you make, teenagers will never be happy with it. I've seen parents give their kids so much freedom. That doesn't work. The irony is that often when those teenagers become adults, they wished their parents had given them some boundaries or a few limits. When mine were little babies and small, I winged it. But, those teenage years were distressing at times and left me doubting everything I ever knew. Still, I must've done something right because both of my children now have good partners.

Nonna

As a baby, I certainly did not win the Trifecta, especially when it came to the three most important footings for a baby to survive. I had no mother, no known father, and no connection to family on either of my parents' sides. I missed out.

But my nights are mostly restful now knowing my new grandson's homelife is the complete opposite to where I came from. He has a wonderful doting mum and dad. Every time I see my grandson he is just flourishing madly with the love and care he receives. He knows me and he calls me Nonna. I insisted that I be called Nonna. His mother said I could not speak Italian, but I said I was Italian and I had the blood disorder to prove it. They agreed on Nonna.

A pandemic has many effects. One of them was missing out on much of my grandson's milestones. My son wanted to be a better parent than myself. I wanted to be a better parent than the orphanage and my mother. We all want to be that much better of a parent when we become parents. I did my best, and I cannot keep whipping myself, considering I was flying solo for so long and also trying to deal with PTSD and enormous amounts of trauma while doing it. I was getting what counselling I could afford and was unable to get free counselling until after the apology in 2009. This might have been too late for my kids to have the full benefit from it. As mentioned, I will always whip myself as it's part of the awful Catholic guilt syndrome. I am recovering and the only reason I walk into a Catholic church these days is to light a candle, or for a funeral.

I know I told my two children how much I loved them, and I kissed them and patched their wounds. I did my best! I can see now that my past has no bearing on either of them as adult children. They are both strong and successful powerhouses. They have it all, and they've worked hard as adults to achieve their own goals. The baton has now been handed over.

I'm overjoyed that my grandson, this little man who turns five soon, has won the daily double with his two devoted parents. The trifecta, quadrella … Parents, grandparents, aunties and uncle, cousins and second cousins on both sides, and a great grandfather Now we have more family to add. He has me and a Nonno, Italian for a great grandfather. I found my very own father, finally breaking the chain of systemic trauma.

Arlo will flourish and prosper. I hope, given the chance, to be an important part of his life, and it's my only real dream to be a loving and present Nonna. Finally, the chain has been broken. It took two generations from my side, and now this new generation has much to look forward to. It's now up to them to hold this new positive banner like a relay race; the race has been won. For myself, I want to sit back and just enjoy this time. It's the autumn of my life. Less stress, less responsibility. I want to keep seeing dreams come true.

2009:
The apology

The apologies for the Stolen Generations took place in 2007 by the then Prime Minister Kevin Rudd. The Forgotten Australians were one year apart. I felt Kevin Rudd was brave to take on such a task, as no other PM had done so. National Sorry Day, or the act of verbalising an apology, saying sorry, is admitting to something. Deprivation of childhood is a dictator of these strange family dynamics. I remember watching the apology for The Stolen Generations on television and thinking about Archie Roach and the lyrics from a song, 'They took the children away.' They did the same to the Forgotten Australians. In more ways than one, we were also taken away. The anger thrown towards these leaders at the time was so abusive. In all fairness, they were not in charge when I was taken. Now, I was decades away from institutional life. It was way behind me, as was this scapegoat role within my family.

Participating in the Senate's inquiry was liberating and

cathartic for me and I am grateful to have been a part of that process. And of course, writing this book. There has been some closure. Regardless of what our views are politically, I thank Kevin 07 for being so brave and finally addressing this poignant issue.

We still have a road ahead of us with the recent Royal Commission and the findings against some of the hierarchy within the Catholic Church finally being held accountable. For now, this is what I want to advocate for and say to the support organizations looking after some of our needs: here is the partial ending of a letter written to Open Place, marking the ten-year apology to the forgotten Australians.

"Let's us, the survivors, mark the ten-year anniversary, and every anniversary, with a minute of peace and silence, so we can send our enduring love to the broken and the fallen, the self-doubters and the triumphant, the survivors! We didn't go to war, our battles were fought not in the battlefield, they were fought in a place deemed safe for babies and small children, children's homes, and institutions."

My name is Kathleen Frances. A moment of silence is all I ask. Never put in the magazine at Open Place.

Vines, and calabria

In 2006, I visited Italy with my friend, Paula. I truly loved Naples, the coastal region. We stayed two days in the Port of Castellammare di Stabia. It was our very first day on tour and we had arrived into a sleeping Stabia. By night, it came alive with little motorbikes zipping around everywhere. This liveliness went on into the early morning hours. We stayed at a cute, classic Italian boutique hotel. In the early hours, I could hear some strange goings-on. Then I was awoken by the elevating alarm that something was wrong. It was a fire alarm. This shrieking crescendo made me fly out of bed, like in the old days at the orphanage. 'Quick,' I said to my friend, 'the place is burning down.'

'Seriously?' she replied in her solemn slumber.

I took her by the arm and led her out the door and down the steps to the bottom floor. On arriving at reception, the only people there were the two of us. The next day, we were informed that a younger Canadian lady on our tour turned out to have bipolar disorder. She was not meant to be drinking alcohol, but she was having a big binge. She had gone off the wagon and was truly on the sauce and her noise was some of what I could hear. It was when she lit a cigarette that the alarms went off. She turned out to be an ongoing situation and was often loud and vocal on the bus. Then, she was mugged in Florence, which delayed our next destination. Being an impatient person, I was finding her a little testing indeed.

Another place we stopped at was Assisi. It had the most breathtaking, untouched, rolling green hills. A place of beauty and isolation. This is where Saint Francis was born. It was here where I purchased a beautiful gold gilded cross. It was my hope that I would one day present this jewel to my biological father when I finally met him. Consequently, I had the cross blessed by an Australian priest in the local basilica. Way before I traced my Italian family, I was already committed by my faith to my lineage on my father's side. I'd always felt a deep spiritual connection to an older woman who would come to me in my dreams, and who I now believe was my Nonna.

For so many years, this woman would gently whisper to me while I lay sleeping, always guiding me, taking my hand in hers, talking to me while my subconscious was saying, don't wake up, stay here, stay where you belong with your olive skin and dark almond eyes. In Naples, I felt an instinctive feeling of alignment. I couldn't explain it and so it's what I call my natural, spiritual instinct. I had this realisation that I was only a few hundred kilometres from where my Nonna was born in Santa Eufemia in Calabria, thirty or more kilometres from a coastal region. My father's people came from the most southern part of the peninsula, and I could visualise my ancestors going back hundreds of years as we stood at the tip of Italy's boot.

I could see how they could've once tended their small vegetable gardens, grown cultivated grapes in the winding cliffs hidden away from strong southern winds overlooking the violet coastline surrounded by the two seas, the Tironian and Ionian. The very poor people who lived here had such simple day-to-day activities. These people were strong and resilient. I could smell Nonna's worn, soft apron with the faded pattern. It had been handwashed with homemade soap from neighbouring olive trees with a slight essence of lavender. Her rough hands held and comforted mine. They made me feel secure and safe in my dreams. Her affirming words were always the same, whether in dreams or in visions. 'I love you, my granddaughter.' Yes, I knew her, and I know of her pain. Life had been harsh. I could tell that she had known sorrow, from the deep lines in her face to the greying hair. She'd also known loss and sadness. She knew love more. She'd embraced this abundance of love in her short, rounded form. Her earthy lineage lives in my every cell, and her blood runs through my veins. Fully inside my third-eye movie, I walk by her side, and enjoy the aromas of basil and fennel, which seem too odoriferous. They are less subtle in scent as she collects herbs and puts them in her pinafore pocket. Now I can see the chickens as they dig and search in the overgrown garden of herbs and weeds and flowers that provide diversity in the landscape. It is here she grabs my hand and puts it in the dirt and makes my hand a fist as I open it. Again, she says, 'You are here.' I can smell the earth, and the oranges as the aroma is carried in the warm tempest air. My senses are overloaded with the feeling of happiness and feeling alive. I can see her kitchen, old and rustic with utensils hanging, instruments of her craft. She lays her pasta down and rolls it through a mangle, layer by layer, and hangs it on wooden perches to dry. She whispers to me before I return to my physical reality. 'Find your family. You are never alone.'

These dreams continued all my life. This gentle female who had seen so much has a strong presence, an inner strength, yet she is warm and emotional. I have seen her tears and her smiles. Her spirit keeps guiding me ahead, forever onwards. I know this woman because she now resides in me. She is my spirit guide, my Nonna.

My papa

I found my biological father at fifty-seven years of age. He was in the very town I was born in. It had been quite the journey. Ancestry DNA led me to the very town I was born in 1962. I found out about the hereditary nature of my kidney disease in 2016. I couldn't stop searching. Surely, I must've been blessed with that for a reason. It was a clue and I was the sleuth. The search slowly started to introduce me to more and more relatives. My Nonna Rosa was correct. I was not alone.

Miraculously, with just one small thread of ancestral twine and a name, I traced down my biological father. The surname was often spelt differently and there was a similarity to the same name, which I had noticed on the big Kenworth trucks I'd seen. When I would see this name, it was like an unease from inside. Intuitively, I always knew. When this name came up more than once on ancestry.com after my DNA had been provided, it all fell into place. With the help from my half-brother, I was guided towards the family of this name in the town where I was born, and eventually to an eighty-five-year-old Calabrian man who'd left Italy after the Second World War in the 1950s.

My biological father had been living in the same town all this time. A town, where I lived as a young married mother. A town I would travel down to see my own daughter and my foster father, Jack. Like the saying goes: it was right under my nose all this time. Being a good natured and respectful woman, I gave my new brother a few months to deliver the news to our father. Months passed, and he just didn't do it. He had done not one but two DNA tests to really clarify that I was his sister. I further found out my brother has an older brother. He was not involved in this testing, and we didn't speak until February 2020. As I had professional experience in my role with assisting clients to find and reconnect with their displaced or lost family, I knew there was a formal process. Once the family had been located, the process included writing a letter from the organisation and sending it. This was a less intrusive way to inform the biological parent or lost siblings. Professionally, this is a much softer introduction, and is less abrasive on the unknowing family member. I put much thought into the scenario of contacting my father. By now, it was clear that my brothers knew I was here, and I began thinking it must've been all too difficult for my half-brother to deal with. In all truth, it was my issue to deal with.

The hard part, which was my main concern, was that there was an innocent party to consider. My father had married his wife, maybe two years after my birth. Being a traditional, Italian man, he went back home and asked a lady he met there to marry him. My father had a wife, and I knew the news would affect her life too; I certainly did not want to hurt anyone. Waiting for either of my brothers to deliver the news was painstakingly slow and drawn out, and I had been holding on to this knowledge of my father for close to a year. The knowledge that he was actually alive, and I wasn't able to access him was heart wrenching. This was not a normal occurrence, and from my own feelings and emotions, this whole situation was life-shifting. I was tremendously close to just showing up to his home. During this time, I consulted with a professional, and my daughter. I decided it would be more polite to write a letter, and maybe follow up with a phone call two weeks later if my brother hadn't spoken to him first. I typed the letter, including my apology for having to deliver such news. Then, my daughter, being less emotionally involved, objectively changed a few things.

'Mum, do not express regret,' she said. 'It's not your fault you were born!' She made it clear to me that I didn't have to be so apologetic. Still, this eighty-five-year-old man was my father, and I would need to try to call him myself. Finally, I plucked up the courage to do this. I called him. It was a very strange experience. Imagine my surprise to hear a very strong Italian accent where it was truly a struggle for us both to communicate. He did promise that it would be better to see each other in person, to which I agreed. Eventually, after waiting for my brother to assist us to somehow come together, I decided to knock on the door. I am so glad I did. I love my Papa so very much. He and I get on so well. We are cut from the same fabric. I cannot believe how we had not had the opportunity to know each other before now. His wife of fifty-seven years is graceful, and we all love her.

My father was into his own viniculture and tended his own grapes. Much of him was still firmly connected to his cultural background. His own history in Italy had been planted in the Australian dirt. Being a romantic dreamer, I had been drawn to grapes, their vines and fruit, since I first noticed the first creeping vine above our home after leaving the orphanage. These little bunches of grapes fascinated my young mind. Watching the golden bees buzzing around these vines made me realise they were special. As a small child, I was already on my journey to becoming a naturalist. The very first career I chose was horticulture, later beekeeping, and for thirty years or more, raising hens.

The garden is another passion of mine. Without a garden there are no bees, and without bees we are truly lost. These passions have lived within me since I first started to walk and looked outwards towards the outside world. Just because I never lived with my father does not mean, inherently, I would not be drawn to things transferred down through my bloodline, pumping through my veins from a family only known to me by my senses. As a child, the very smell of things would leave me in a dreamlike state, calm and feeling safe. Lavender and rosemary and roses. The smell of the ocean while on holidays. That truly awakened who I was. I was a coastal girl through my ancestral threads.

I believed this Calabrian man was definitely my father genetically, but would he have that emotional connection? As we get older, we need these important ancestral blueprints to help us stay connected in some way to our roots. To make wine with my own father would be an absolute dream come true for me. I hadn't heard from him, and I knew I should let go, because the fear of more abandonment was so overwhelming.

My need to know him was as strong as my love for my kids and grandson. I had not come this far in my life to give up on my grandmother invading my dreams or to not experience rejection one more time. I leant into some honesty and I went and I knocked on their door. I had to reveal myself. I had to see the other side of the coin. I had to have come from a different, and stronger lineage. My looks, my nature, they were all too different from my mother, and her mother, and my half-sisters.

I may not have grown up with him, but I am very much like him. This is our DNA, but there is also a different blueprint that is passed down through our DNA. The body has a memory. Chemical caps on our DNA can leave behind memories. There are studies now about past traumas and memories being passed down, and this theory relates to my happy memories and my dreams about my Italian Nonna. My Nonna Rosa was with me from birth. I look like her. I look like my father.

When it comes to my father, I was in fact his first born and his only daughter. I knew I had inherited my authentic love of the soil and nature from my Nonna. When visiting Italy in 2006, I took a few cooking classes and learned to make eggplant parmigiana and some real Italian sauces, like Basil Sugo, the base passata, with onion, basil, celery, carrots, and olive oil. One day, I will learn to make wine in the village Santa Eufemia in Calabria. There is a large palm tree in the coat of arms of Palmi. Their patron saint is Nicholas. His birthday is the same day as my grandson, Arlo. When I get there, I'll walk to the top where the three large, white crosses look out onto the Violet Coast, out on to the sparkling sea. This will happen for me, and I know that Nonna will be there in spirit. She is there to guide me. I will visit some of the places out of the wonderful book I read called *My Brilliant Friend* by Elena Ferrante. After this, I will visit Messina in Sicily.

When I think of the women I've known in my waking hours and in my dreams, like Nonna, they are the true strength of this story. Women who are faced with so many ongoing losses, and yet continue to find resilience and still, without little or no support, keep true to themselves. My Nonna's three sons and daughter left for distant shores. She knew loss, as I have known it. Different, but in a way, similar. For my immediate family, we have one thing in common. We have been a fatherless society. All the men in our lives left and abandoned us. Through tragic deaths, or by choice, they were gone. My trip to Italy will be from a feminine perspective, and I will seek the guidance of the wise women to help me achieve my dreams. 'Come again,' they both said. I was courageous. They made me welcome, and I faced that fear of rejection.

I could've wasted another year waiting, but I did not; I embraced the present, we had a three-year anniversary last week. My Papa told me that years ago, I knocked on his door, and then he learned he had a beautiful daughter. There is one thing that worries me a lot. I lean into the honest truth often. I frequently wondered if he had some idea that I was born. The town I was born in was very microcosmic, especially back in the 1960s. The population was twelve thousand people.

He would have seen my pregnant mother. I was born in May, 1962 and was taken away six months later.

Occasionally, I think if this was the case, he was as scared as my mother of divulging the truth. Men did not plan to be with women very often back then. They were not in love. It was a friendship. What I do know is that he hates any kind of confrontation. He has a kind-hearted nature. He would never want to let anyone down.

Prior to meeting his devoted wife in 1963, he did not need a scandal or to change his planned pathway. I still have a question mark in my head. What man would have dealt with this situation in 1962? No man, I believe.

His older brother by eleven years, Joe, really tried in many ways to guide and be a dad to my Papa. They lost their own father in 1938. He left a wife and seven little children behind. One was only six months old. What a tragedy for them and my Nonna. His brother Giovani was already married before he came to Australia. He tried to keep a short lead on my Papa. Joe did warn my father to behave as an older brother. My Papa was a very good looking and athletic man, quite the catch in his day. Papa loved his family and would never want to bring any shame or embarrassment to them in Australia or in Calabria. I will never know the honest truth. All I know is that I never got in the way. He completed the Italian cycle. He went home to Italy met a beautiful younger lady and got married. He had his home, his business that they worked hard to build up, two sons, who were good providers and worked late and at all hours. It was not easy for them. My Papa loves being an Australian; he is a citizen. I still feel the relationship we have is better than good. It is fantastic. We have a lifetime of things in common; my love of the earth is one we share.

When I see him, I see myself. When I see my son, his grandson, with his Nonno, I see my Papa. Looking like him and my Nonna helps, I am sure. He said when he left Italy his mother looked similar to what I look like now. Now I know him, I will never leave him. He loves me, and I love him dearly. I do have lots of family. Brothers, Concetta, cousins and it goes on. They are all good people. I thank the angels in heaven for this chance to not only find myself but to admire the strength that came in my DNA from both sides of the coin. It's wonderful to see my grown kids see their Italian Nonno and for my father to know his great-grandson, and Arlo knows he has an Italian granddad too.

THE END

*With my papa finally we are making
many special memories together*

Afterword
Random Acts of Kindness

These days, I call myself a fully salvaged recovered Catholic. The Catholic Church manufactured many things, but love was never one of them. I finally drew this conclusion after my many experiences that left me with no faith in a church with such a long history of judgements, abuses, and sadness. Jesus did not live between the walls of the orphanage. He was love and all things good. Even outside of my orphanage life, I still was subject to humiliation throughout my Catholic school education. The most humiliating situation came in grade five or six. I was so isolated during lunch times and was always being teased and called nicknames. I felt like I never fit in anywhere. Many times, I avoided the taunts made by children in the school yard. When this happened, and it did, regularly, I headed into the church to pray for a nice life. I had a philosophical nature, was an optimist, and this was my time away from all of the excessive sensory participation. Suffering from dyslexia was, and still is, absolutely exhausting. Sensory overload would make me go into a dream-like state. Total overload is a stage where no matter how many times something is explained to you, you just sit there with a blank look. This is not just a façade; it's the external manifestation of being debilitated by overwhelm.

Inside the church, there was a small walled-off side area attached not far away from the confessional boxes. I attended these booths often enough. While sitting there, queued in line with the other children, I often wondered if they too were making up something worthy of penance. Sins ranged from getting angry at my little sister to picking roses hanging over from the kindergarten fence. After all, anything hanging over was deemed fair game, wasn't it?

Still, my conscience always reminded me I was a sinner. You'd start your repentance with the well-known verse: 'Forgive me Father, for I have sinned.' After repenting, you'd be assigned a few Hail Marys and Our Fathers, and then slip on the dark side of the road again. The room was planned as a place of reflection and atonement. It came in handy for those big Italian overflowing funerals with all of their full requiem masses that needed extra room. At Catholic school, this room was where I sat to escape my daily torment in the playground. On an unusually quiet day, I stumbled on a beautiful white bible. I soon realised it was our local parish priest's personal bible. Curiosity killed the cat, as they say. I began looking through its gold leaf pages. I gathered it was a gift from the priest's mother, perhaps given to him when he'd left the seminary as there was a younger photo of himself and of his mother, who resembled his round, stern, unemotional face. She looked like the female version of him. I knew he was Irish as he had a soft Irish brogue, and, yet, he seemed fierce and strong. He always had black rings under his eyes. They looked right through you.

During his sermons, if he glanced your way, it left you feeling worried or slightly uneasy. Could it be he was trying to remind you that you'd been bad and he was letting you in on what God had told him about you? While I was pondering about him being just as human as all the other parishioners, he came in and caught me snooping in his bible. He looked at me sternly, so I commented on what a beautiful bible he had. Still, I was sprung, and I handed the book to the rightful owner. There it was, another thing to confess in the confessional box. It was not so hard to pluck up sins. I was collecting them like a daisy chain. Is this a sin? Ten points it is? Or, two points? No? Let it go? The Catholic Church created the words, guilt and shame. They were the manufacturers of guilt. If you attended church habitually and put your money in the collection box each Sunday, you had a one-way ticket to heaven. If you didn't, you were going to hell in a hand basket. Seemed like I'd been a terrible sinner, as both Father C. and the principal, Sister Mary, decided I would not be making my confirmation. Sister Mary announced it to my whole class. She said I was not ready for this important Holy Sacrament. I was gutted and disgraced beyond possibility.

Never once did she sit me down and ask how my life was at home? More social isolation followed after that at school. Out of twenty-five children I was considered to not be ready to accept God. Not only did this cause retribution at school, life at home was another issue. To this day, I still have my own faith in the things that are gentle and caring and safe. As they say, 'When something has ended, I'm done!' As for quiet times of reflection, I still have them in my own company. Meditation and gratitude for the small mercies are far more precious. This mindset assists me to pay it forward more often. There is a lot said for generosity of spirit and how we might do this quietly with no bells and whistles.

I felt by writing my experiences down that I might be able to help many readers who know, or have known, what it feels like to be emotionally tired or exhausted. It was my intention for my story to challenge readers by showing them that even though my life has not always been easy, my past experiences do not affect my every mood or define who I am today. By changing my perception and seeing that I am not a victim, I have a say in how my life plays out. I have a choice in everything I do. My life has been a journey of resilience. While writing this story, I've been able to recognise my many strengths. Yes, I have at times lost much, including the loss of childhood and simply enjoying being a teenager, if that's possible. My life has been one of endurance and an innate strength, and I can only speak for myself, but this outlook has helped me to not only do the internal work, but have a sustainable career and life.

I will let you in on a little secret. Every week, I do voluntary work. Well, that's what I call it. It's a choice I make to do it. No one knows I do it, not even my kids. But, I've been doing random acts of kindness for a long time now. I take time out to help someone each week, or daily, depending on whatever's going on. Usually, with most of my chosen and personal time, I work with many people I don't know. It's a pay it forward kind of thing. It lifts my spirits and it's so nice to see strangers having a surprised look and smiling back. I do not take dangerous risks, as that would defeat the purpose. But, it's lovely having the power to make a difference. It's not always a monetary exchange. Many of the things I do are completely simplistic and easy. You do not have to martyr yourself by doing this, or sacrifice your own family or needs. Just a small thing makes a huge difference. For example, just by exchanging a flower bulb or snipping from your garden, or offering your shopping trolley to an elderly person, it all makes a huge difference in their life.

For instance, a few weeks ago, I couldn't get my usual hairdresser, as she was flat out. I desperately needed to get my hair done for a wedding, so I rocked to one of those cheap haircut salons, you know the ones where you just sit down and wait your turn. So, I observed this young girl working hard and intuitively, I knew she would pick me as her next customer. As I sat down and she coloured my hair, she started to ask me what I did for work? I told her I had nearly twenty-five years in community services. Homelessness, mental health, and so on. It was then she told me she wanted to set her career pathway also into social science. That was the connection. There are no ordinary moments. Briefly, we chatted and she moved onto her other client and then came back to wash my colour out. She had studied extensively, but for many reasons, was hooked into a job that was just paying the bills and she needed some vocational advice. I decided to pass her my number and see if she would follow up. She did, and I mapped out some concrete ideas. Knowing all the services and having many contacts in the field, I made a few calls. I wrote a few ideas out, and then she was ready to apply for a position. I also assisted her with some examples of how to answer the job criteria on the application.

The way to feel better about yourself is often by doing just one selfless thing once a week. It doesn't have to be an all-day thing. My next helpful task is to assist an elderly lady to downsize and take some unwanted things to the thrift shop. When I walk away, I always feel a nice buzz and a sense of contentment. Whilst recognising someone else's needs within these scenarios, I always find reason for my own existence. There are many other things that have helped me through some awfully tough times. A sense of humour has assisted me to remain sane. Trauma needs to be addressed because, like running from a crashing wave while wading in the ocean, it will hit you. And, if you choose to bury it, it will hit you harder than ever. Talking about it in a safe setting assists you to unpack the traumatic experiences, one by one, until the traumatic response has no emotional impact on you. It's like there is a middle ground, the balance where the pendulum gravitates to the dead centre.

It's not healthy for a person to remain in a euphoric state. Happiness is not a continual state we need to be in. We need to not be in a low depressive mood either, not for too long. So, it's finding your own individual middle ground. This takes practice and some soul searching. For myself, I find this place by reading or watching or listening to podcasts and stories. These are what 'work' when it comes to my own journey. I never take too much on, as it can leave me feeling psychologically spent. As much as I enjoy company, I will not sacrifice my own health if I'm around an emotional vampire.

You will know one or two of these because when you leave them you feel worn out and brain dead.

Also, when rendering assistance, they are usually up for their next drama. People who live this lifestyle often seem to invite or attract negativity. Patterns are something we all have to be aware of. Like Freddy Mercury sings, 'I want to break free,' we must acknowledge and do the work to break free. With creative visualization you will break free. Humans are very complex beings; we can allude ourselves to make changes in our lives to start with because often these changes initially come to us as loss. Often others around you won't always be happy for you if you're making changes that inadvertently challenge them in some way. The tribe you're hanging with now may not be the tribe you hang out with once the changes have occurred. You will find a new tribe, or clan, one that is also based on your energy, and if it's positive energy, you will attract positive folk into your life.

I have heard many say, 'fake it until you make it.' That's fine, but it's extremely unhealthy to ignore anxieties and depression. It's important to acknowledge the past with the appropriate professionals alongside you to assist the forward movement. Just recently, I watched a well-known expert talking about depression and trauma. To use an illustration of what this might feel like, an example was used by filling up a very large, tall vase or jar.

The first layer put in was orange lentils. Perhaps this was the loss of a pet, while watching it get hit by a car. The second layer was of kidney beans, symbolising perhaps getting bullied daily at school or fearing what the day might bring. Then, a few more layers were added using coloured objects, maybe a death of someone close, a grandparent, an adult existing through an abusive relationship, etc. Eventually, the jar starts to overflow. This is an easy way of visualising trauma. This is how I experienced PTSD and depression. When someone who has no idea about trauma tells you that 'you need to fake it until you make it,' tell them to hush and leave them in their small world.

My understanding of recovery is by addressing trauma, you can look at the trigger. It's possible to look at other forms of desensitisations, if you have a fear of something. I have seen a grown man scale a car because he was scared of chickens. I have known people who won't step on a plane due to fear. One time, I worked with a lady who would turn to jelly if she saw a monkey spider. To the sufferers, these fears are real. Working on fear is so brave and so empowering. 'Fake it 'till you make it' is not a healthy perspective. Face your fears with support and there will be fewer limits on your life. I use creative visualization, and for me this is an empowering tool for moving forward without limits.

www.ingramcontent.com/pod-product-compliance
Lightning Source LLC
Chambersburg PA
CBHW030050100526
44591CB00008B/86